Grade 7 | Module 3

➤ STUDENT JOURNAL

Paths to College and Career

English Language Arts

Understanding Perspectives

Cover design by Wiley

Published by Jossey-Bass
A Wiley Brand
One Montgomery Street, Suite 1000, San Francisco, CA 94104-4594—www.josseybass.com

Jossey-Bass books and products are available through most bookstores. To contact Jossey-Bass directly call our Customer Care Department within the U.S. at 800-956-7739, outside the U.S. at 317-572-3986, or fax 317-572-4002.

Wiley publishes in a variety of print and electronic formats and by print-on-demand. Some material included with standard print versions of this book may not be included in e-books or in print-on-demand. If this book refers to media such as a CD or DVD that is not included in the version you purchased, you may download this material at http://booksupport.wiley.com. For more information about Wiley products, visit www.wiley.com.

ISBN: 978-1-119-10516-9

Printed in the United States of America

FIRST EDITION

PB Printing 10 9 8 7 6 5 4

CONTENTS

Unit 3 191

EXPEDITIONARY
LEARNING

Powerful Stories Anchor Chart

What Gives Stories Their Enduring Power?

Powerful stories and language make you feel something or change your thinking.

Story or Poem	Content	Theme	Language	Images
The People Could Fly	The text or passage slavery	lesson the reader can learn the man was teaching them to fly but really dieying	the words used to say something wait for your turn to die	Pictures when the man had whip the baby
Narrative of the Life of Frederick Douglass, chapters 1 and 2				
"Negro Speaks of Rivers"				
Last Day of Slavery				

Powerful Story Note-Catcher

Name: Darion Bell

Date: ______________________

Directions: After each selection from the story is read aloud, talk with your peer about what words and images you found powerful. Record your thinking on the following chart.

Page	What is a phrase or sentence that you think is powerful? Write it on the paper and explain what it helps you understand or how it makes you feel.	What about the image is powerful? Tell which part of the image you are looking at and explain what it helps you understand or how it makes you feel.
5	the man had hit the baby	
7	the man who was flying was teaching them to fly but really to die	
9		
10		

Finally, talk with your peer about what you think the theme of this story is. Record your ideas below.

What do you think the theme of *The People Could Fly* is?

____

____

____

Remember:

A *theme* of a book is the message or the lesson that the author is trying to convey.

- It is a statement that is broadly applicable to situations beyond the story.

Entry Task

Introduction to Module 3

Name: Darion Bell

Date: Jan 9, 2018

Directions: Please look closely at the book covers. Then answer the following questions.

1. What do you see? How do these images differ?

2. Which one of these covers makes you most interested in reading this book? Why?

3. What might this book be about?

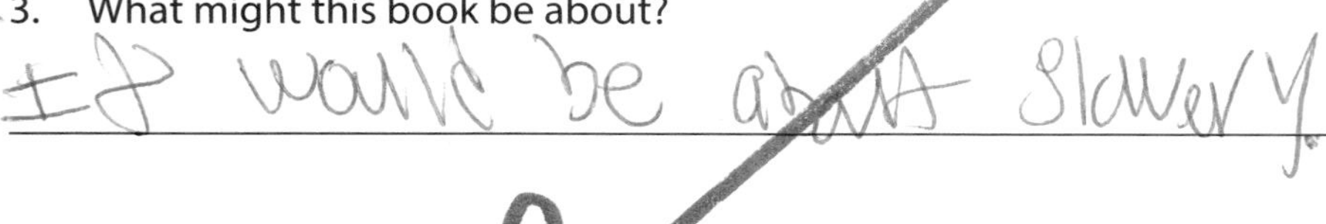

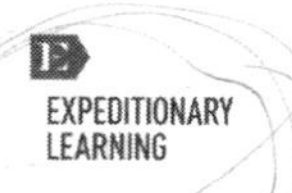

Gallery Walk Directions

Name: ____

Date: ____

Step 1. On My Own

Directions: Silently walk around the classroom and look at the different gallery items. At each item, consider the following questions:

What do you notice?

- How might this relate to the central text?
- How does my idea relate to someone else's?
- Using the sticky notes provided, place your answers on the paper next to the item.

Step 2. With My Group

Directions:

1. Read through the ideas placed by your classmates. Then discuss these questions and record your ideas on this sheet:
   - In which box (including the center one) on the Historical Context Anchor Chart would you place this item? Why?
   - Based on this item, what can you predict about the central text or its context?
2. After you have heard the groups report out, annotate your Historical Context Anchor Chart to indicate how each of the three boxes relates to the central text.

EXPEDITIONARY LEARNING

Suggested Gallery Walk Items

Item A: "slaveships"

Source: Clifton, Lucille. "slaveships." The Collected Poems of Lucille Clifton. *Copyright © 1996 by Lucille Clifton. Reprinted with permission of The Permissions Company, Inc., on behalf of BOA Editions Ltd., www.boaeditions.org.*

loaded like spoons

into the belly of Jesus

where we lay for weeks for months

in the sweat and stink of our own

breathing

—from "slaveships" by Lucille Clifton

Item B: Map showing slave and free states before the Civil War (circa 1850)

Teacher created: Do an Internet search or use a copy of the social studies textbook at your school.

Item C: Picture of slaves in a cotton field

Source: Hubbard and Mix, "Cotton field, Retreat Plantation, Port Royal Island, S.C.," 1860. http://www.loc.gov/pictures/item/2012648060/.

Item D: Quote from *Narrative of the Life of Frederick Douglass*

Source: Douglass, Frederick. Narrative of the Life of Frederick Douglass. *Boston, Massachusetts: Anti-Slavery Office, 1845. Project Gutenberg. http://www.gutenberg.org/files/23/23-h/23-h.htm.*

> "There were no beds given the slaves, unless one coarse blanket be considered such, and none by the men and women had these. This, however, is not considered a very great privation. They find less difficulty from the want of beds, than from the want of time to sleep . . . when this [work] is done, old and young, male and female, married and single, drop down side by side, on one common bed,—the cold, damp floor,—each covering himself or herself with their miserable blankets; and here they sleep until they are summoned to the field by the driver's horn. . . . Mr. Severe, the overseer, use to stand by the door of the quarter, armed with a large hickory stick and heavy cowskin, ready to whip anyone who was so unfortunate as not to hear, or, from any other cause, was prevented from being ready to start for the field at the sound of the horn."

Item E: Quote from *Narrative of the Life of Frederick Douglass*

Source: Douglass, Frederick. Narrative of the Life of Frederick Douglass. *Boston, Massachusetts: Anti-Slavery Office, 1845. Project Gutenberg. http://www.gutenberg.org/files/23/23-h/23-h.htm.*

> "I have been frequently asked how I felt when I found myself in a free State. I have never been able to answer the question with any satisfaction to myself. It was a moment of the highest excitement I ever experienced. I suppose I felt as one may imagine the unarmed mariner to feel when he is rescued by a friendly man-of-war from the pursuit of a pirate. . . . I felt like one who had escaped a den of hungry lions."

Item F: Copy of *North Star,* the abolitionist newspaper Frederick Douglass published

Source: The North Star, First Edition, December 3, 1847, Rochester, NY (MSA SC 5557, M13,053). Editors Frederick Douglass and Martin R. Delaney, Publisher William C. Nell. http://www.loc.gov/exhibits/odyssey/archive/02/0210001r.jpg.

Sam'l Brooks

THE NORTH STAR.

RIGHT IS OF NO SEX—TRUTH IS OF NO COLOR—GOD IS THE FATHER OF US ALL, AND ALL WE ARE BRETHREN.

VOL. I. NO. 23. ROCHESTER, N. Y., FRIDAY, JUNE 2, 1848. WHOLE NO.—23.

Communication.

Selections.

EXPEDITIONARY LEARNING

Item G: Defense of slavery

Source: Fitzhugh, George. "The Universal Law of Slavery." Africans in America. 1857. Public Domain.

> "He the Negro is but a grown up child, and must be governed as a child, not as a lunatic or criminal. The master occupies toward him the place of a parent or guardian."
>
> "The negro race is inferior to the white race, and living in their midst, they would be far outstripped or outwitted in the chaos of free competition."
>
> "Our negroes are not only better off as to physical comfort than free laborers, but their moral condition is better."

Item H: American Anti-Slavery Society Convention, 1840

Source: "The Abolition of the Slave Trade" (The Anti-Slavery Society Convention, 1840) circa 1846–1864. © National Portrait Gallery, London. http://www.npg.org.uk/collections/search/portraitLarge/mw84907/The-Abolition-of-the-Slave-Trade-The-Anti-Slavery-Society-Convention-1840.

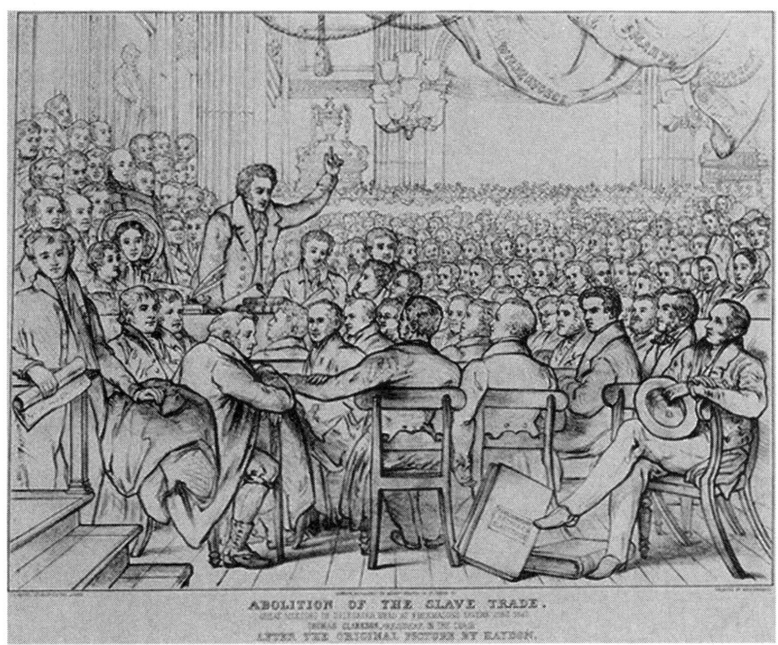

Historical Context Anchor Chart

Slavery	Debate over Slavery
Slavery is a bad place were black people work for white people.	why do the slave master have to use black people to do there biding.

Life of Frederick Douglass
he want to stop slavery and he writes about it so that he want everybody to here his story and history.

Vocabulary
Slavery Douglass

NARRATIVE OF THE LIFE OF FREDERICK DOUGLASS

by Frederick Douglass

EXPEDITIONARY
LEARNING

Module 3 Guiding Questions

What gives stories and songs their enduring power?

How did Douglass's purpose and audience shape how he told his story?

EXPEDITIONARY
LEARNING

Vocabulary: "The Slave Trade" and "Abolition"

Name: ______________________________

Date: ______________________________

Directions: In class, we read several texts. Knowing the terms in this table helps you better understand these texts. Read the definitions, and underline or highlight key words in each definition.

Vocabulary	Definition
triangular slave trade	(n.) A trading system between three ports. The best-known triangular trading system is the transatlantic slave trade that operated from the late 16th to early 19th centuries, carrying slaves, cash crops, and manufactured goods between West Africa, American colonies, and the European colonial powers.
abolitionist	(n.) A person who believed in and often fought for the end of slavery.
system	(n.) A set of things working together as parts of a whole or an interconnecting network, such as the slavery system in the United States.
enforced labor	(n.) Work that someone does against his or her will.
plantation	(n.) A large field that is used to grow crops, such as tobacco, cotton, and sugar.
crops	(n.) Plants that are planted, grown, and often sold.
racial inequality	(n.) Also known as racism; discrimination based on race that affects the opportunities an individual can get.

Directions: Fill in the blanks in the paragraph by using each word once. Check off each word you use to help you keep track of what is left.

- ☐ Triangular slave trade
- ☐ Abolitionist
- ☐ System
- ☐ Enforced labor
- ☐ Plantation
- ☐ Crops
- ☐ Racial inequality

Slaves were brought over from Africa through the __triangular slave trade__. Slaves were bought for cash __crops__, such as cotton, sugar, and tobacco, which were traded in England for manufactured goods, such as rum and guns. The __enforced or labor__ of slaves made white Southern __Plantion__ owners a lot of money. Many slave owners also believed in __in racil inequality__ and thought slaves were inferior to whites because of the color of their skin. They used this reasoning to justify their harsh treatment of African Americans. Although there were many in the South who economically benefited from slavery, Frederick Douglass was a famous __abolitionist__ who fought for the end of slavery. A former slave himself, he witnessed the horrors of the __systen__ firsthand.

Answers for Vocabulary Homework

Slaves were brought over from Africa through the triangular slave trade. Slaves were bought for cash crops, such as cotton, sugar, and tobacco, which were traded in England for manufactured goods, such as rum and guns. The enforced labor of slaves made white Southern plantation owners a lot of money. Many slave owners also believed in racial inequality and thought slaves were inferior to whites because of the color of their skin. They used this reasoning to justify their harsh treatment of African Americans. Although there were many in the South who economically benefited from slavery, Frederick Douglass was a famous abolitionist who fought for the end of slavery. A former slave himself, he witnessed the horrors of the system firsthand.

Analyzing Images: Slavery in America

Name: Darion Bell

Date: Jan 10 2018

Focus Questions

- Why did slavery exist?
- How did slaves come to the United States?
- What was life like for enslaved Americans?

Today, you will analyze a series of images related to slavery and the slave trade. Look at each image carefully and note what you see. Then draw conclusions, trying to answer the focus questions.

The images are all in the image browser associated with PBS: *History of Webisode 5* resources and can be found at: http://www.pbs.org/wnet/historyofus/tools/browser5.html. Please note that you will only use some of the images. The text next to each image provides important information.

Image	I observe . . .	I conclude that . . .
Slave Ship	to see a box.	Put it togethe or add it slaves are not happy.
A Virginia Slave Group	the slaves are in prison.	I conclude that they want to be free.
Slaves in a Cotton Field	I see they are working in crops.	I conclude that they want to stop working.
A Slave's Whip Marks	I see that the slave gots whiped.	I conclude that why do the get whiped for doing there jobs. for them.

"The Slave Trade"

Text from *Freedom: A History of US,* Webisode 5

Source: http://www.pbs.org/wnet/historyofus/web05/segment2.html.

1. Slavery first came to America with some of the earliest settlers. But they weren't the first people to own human beings. Slavery was an evil found around the world. There were jobs no one wanted to do, and, in the days before machinery, slaves seemed an answer. If you were on the losing side of a war, or were kidnapped by a rival tribe or a thief, you might end up a slave. Some Native Americans owned slaves. It was an ancient practice in Africa. But slavery in Africa was a **domestic institution**. In America it would go way beyond that, developing into a system of enforced labor on vast plantations. And while in Africa blacks were owned by other blacks, in America blacks were always owned by whites. In America it would always be racial slavery.

2. By the eighteenth century there had developed a special pattern to the American slave trade. New England Yankees often started it by taking their salted cod to the Caribbean island of Barbados—just north of Venezuela. There they traded the fish for cane sugar. Then they headed back north to Virginia where they loaded tobacco before sailing east across the Atlantic to England. In England the cargo was exchanged for guns and cloth and trinkets—all of which could be used to buy human beings in Africa. Then the slave ships sailed south from England to Africa to fill their holds with African men, women, and children—who were the most valuable cargo of all. Those people sailed west—against their wishes—and were usually taken to a Caribbean island or a southern port where the sea captains sold them for cash or more sugar. Finally, the crisscrossed triangular journey ended in Massachusetts or New York or Annapolis. Robert Walsh was an **eyewitness** of a slave ship in action. He wrote: "The slaves were all enclosed under grated hatchways, between decks. The space was so low they sat between each other's legs . . . [and] there was no possibility of lying down, or at all changing their position, by night or day. Over the hatchway stood a ferocious-looking fellow with a **scourge** of many twisted thongs in his hand, who was the slavedriver of the ship. . . . The last parting sounds we heard from the unhallowed ship were the cries and shrieks of the slaves, suffering under some bodily **affliction**."

3. In Colonial times, there was slavery in both North and South. But slavery didn't make much sense in the North; farms were small and the farmer could often handle the work himself. The situation was different in the South. The crops that grew well there—tobacco, cotton, rice, and sugar—demanded large numbers of field workers. But there were few workers to be had—until the advent of African slavery.

4. By 1700 tens of thousands of African-born blacks are living in the American South, and the numbers are fast increasing. In 1705, in Virginia laws are passed that attempt to take away slaves' humanity. The Virginia Black Code says slaves are property, not people. But property that can think means trouble. So laws are passed to try to prevent thinking. One North Carolina law read this way: "The teaching of slaves has a tendency to **excite** dissatisfaction in their minds. Therefore, any free person

who shall teach any slave to read and write shall be **liable to indictment**. If any slave shall teach, or attempt to teach, any other slave, he or she shall receive thirty-nine lashes on his or her bare back."

5. When you do something you know is wrong, you usually try to convince yourself that it really is all right. Southerners begin to say that God created some people to be slaves and some to be masters. They say black people aren't as smart as white people. Then, to make that true, they pass laws that say it is a crime to teach blacks to read and write. One white woman in Norfolk, Virginia, who teaches free blacks in her home, is arrested and put in jail. Whites are losing their freedom too.

Definitions

Domestic: related to or based in the household

Institution: a system for organizing society that has existed for a long time

Eyewitness: someone who saw something themselves

Scourge: whip

Affliction: something that causes pain or suffering

Excite: create or stir up

Liable to indictment: able to be charged with a crime

EXPEDITIONARY LEARNING

Text-Dependent Questions

"The Slave Trade"

Questions	Answers
Answer the questions in complete sentences. Notice that the answer to the second question should be 3–4 sentences long.	
In Paragraph 2 1. What were the three main steps involved in the triangular slave trade?	they traded fish for sugar, next the are going to sail sugar for labors
In Paragraph 2 2. What were conditions like on the slave ships? Support your answer with evidence from the text.	The conditions on the slave were ruff and different by the eighteen
In Paragraphs 3 and 4 3. Why were there so many more slaves in the South than the North? 4. Why did the Black Codes prohibit teaching slaves to read and write?	They had to work for them.
In Paragraph 5 5. How did some Southerners use racial differences to justify slavery?	They been doing drugs so they they get slaves.

"Abolition"

Text from *Freedom: A History of US,* Webisode 5

Source: http://www.pbs.org/wnet/historyofus/web05/segment3.html.

1. Abolition! Back in 1765 Americans had shouted the word. Before the Revolution it was the hated British stamp tax the colonists wanted to **abolish**. Then the word began to be used with a new meaning. It was the slave trade some wanted to abolish, and then slavery itself. In 1775 Benjamin Franklin helped found the American Abolition Society. The Constitution said the slave trade could be officially ended in 1808. When Thomas Jefferson becomes president, he reminds everyone of that, and a law is passed ending the slave trade. Now, no additional people can be enslaved—at least not legally. An elated Jefferson said this: "I congratulate you, fellow citizens, on the approach of the period at which you may **interpose** your authority **constitutionally** to withdraw the citizens of the United States from all further participation in those violations of human rights which have been so long continued on the unoffending inhabitants of Africa."

2. But ending the international slave trade doesn't put an end to slavery itself, which continues to grow by **natural increase**. And within the South a major internal slave trade develops. Many thinking people—both Northerners and Southerners—believe slavery is morally wrong. Yet few are willing to do anything about it. Slavery is a profitable way of life. Those who do speak out—the abolitionists—aren't very popular. Many people argue that if slavery is abolished it will wreck the Southern economy. James Henry Hammond was one of them. He said, "Do you imagine you could prevail on us to give up a thousand million dollars in the value of our slaves, and a thousand million more in the value of our lands?"

3. The Southern leaders don't seem to understand. Immigrants and ideas and inventions are beginning to change the North. The South will be left out of much of that excitement. The Frenchman Alexis de Tocqueville visits the United States and observes a free state and a slave state. He writes about what he sees: "On the north bank of the Ohio, everything is activity, industry; labor is honored; there are no slaves. Pass to the south bank and the scene changes so suddenly that you think yourself on the other side of the world; the **enterprising** spirit is gone."

4. And yet still, because of the huge importance of cotton, the South remains the wealthiest part of the nation. Both North and South are jealous of political power. Each wants to dominate the government in Washington. But as long as Congress is evenly divided between slave states and free states, there is some stability. Then, in 1820, Missouri asks to enter the Union as a slave state. Northerners are alarmed. If Missouri becomes a state, the North will be outvoted in Congress. What can be done? Finally, a solution is found. Maine is carved from Massachusetts and made into a state, a free state. That keeps the balance of free and slave states. At the same time, the territories north of Missouri's southern border are to remain free. That action is called the Missouri Compromise. It keeps North and South talking to each other, but just barely. In 1845 slave owner James Hammond writes this to an abolitionist. He says: "I **repudiate**, as ridiculously absurd, that much lauded dogma of Mr. Jefferson that 'all men are born equal.' No society has ever yet existed without a natural

variety of classes. Slavery is truly the cornerstone and foundation of every well-designed and durable republican **edifice**."

5. Meanwhile, Mr. Hammond and his planter friends are falling out of step with the European world. There, in the first half of the nineteenth century, most nations outlaw slavery. The Europeans begin to criticize the United States for allowing it. There are also white Northerners who are increasingly speaking out against slavery. By 1840 there are said to be about 2,000 abolitionist societies in the North. While some talk of gradually freeing the slaves and even paying the owners the cash value of their slaves, most abolitionists don't think anyone should be paid for owning anyone else. They want to end slavery—bam—just like that—and too bad for the slave owners. William Lloyd Garrison, a white man from Massachusetts, is the founder of the American Anti-Slavery Society and the publisher of the leading abolitionist newspaper, *The Liberator.* He says, "I do not wish to think, or speak, or write with **moderation**. No! Tell a man whose house is on fire, to give a moderate alarm, but urge me not to use moderation in a cause like the present. I am in earnest—I will not retreat a single inch—and I WILL BE HEARD."

Definitions

Abolish: to officially end a law or system

Interpose: to put oneself between two things

Constitutionally: in agreement with the Constitution

Natural increase: when a population grows because more people are born

Enterprising: able to think of and carry out new ideas

Repudiate: deny, reject

Edifice: building

Moderation: within reasonable limits, not calling for extreme action

EXPEDITIONARY LEARNING

Text-Dependent Questions, Part 1

"Abolition"

Name: Darion Bell

Date: Jan 11, 2018

Directions: Read the "Abolition" text. Then answer the following questions.

Questions	Answers
Paragraph 1 1. How did the slave trade end?	It was the slave some wanted to abolish.
Paragraph 2 2. What does morally wrong mean? Given what you learned yesterday, what would someone who argued that slavery was morally wrong say about why slavery should end?	slavery is a profitable way of life.
Paragraph 2 3. What did James Henry Hammond think about ending slavery? Underline three words or phrases in the text that support your answer.	slavery itself which continues to grow by natural increase.
Paragraph 4 4. Why does having new states join the Union cause disagreement between the Northern and Southern states? 5. What was the Missouri Compromise and why was it important? 6. What would James Henry Hammond say about whether or not slavery should end?	South are jealous of cotton, the south remains the weathiest part of the nation
Paragraph 5 7. What did European countries decide about slavery? 8. What is the debate in the abolition movement over how slavery should end?	European word there in the first half of the nineteenth.

Historical Context Anchor Chart

Name: ______________________________

Date: ______________________________

Slavery	**Debate over Slavery**

Life of Frederick Douglass

Vocabulary	
Triangular slave trade	*Plantation*
Abolitionist	*Crops*
System	*Racial inequality*
Enforced labor	

Text-Dependent Questions, Part 2

"Abolition"

Name: ______________________________

Date: ______________________________

Directions: Answer the following questions. Each answer should be at least 2–3 sentences and should include evidence from the text.

Questions	Answers
1. What is the difference between ending the slave trade and ending slavery?	
2. Those who defended slavery used various arguments. In the text, Hammond is quoted twice. What two reasons does he give in arguing that slavery should continue?	
3. What argument is Garrison making in the last paragraph? How does this quote connect to the wide agreement among abolitionists that slavery should end immediately and without compensation for slave owners?	

EXPEDITIONARY LEARNING

"Frederick Douglass"

Text from *Freedom: A History of US,* Webisode 5

(Assessment Text)

Source: http://www.pbs.org/wnet/historyofus/web05/segment4.html.

1. In 1841, a runaway slave, a tall, handsome man named Frederick Douglass, speaks up at an abolitionist meeting on Nantucket Island, near Boston: "I felt strongly moved to speak. But the truth was, I felt myself a slave, and the idea of speaking to white people weighed me down."
2. Yet he finds the courage to speak out. Frederick Douglass just tells his own story: how he has lived and what he had seen. That is enough to send chills down the backs of his listeners. "I never saw my mother more than four or five times in my life," he says. "She made her journeys to see me in the night, traveling the whole distance on foot (twelve miles), after the performance of her day's work. She was a field hand, and a whipping is the penalty of not being in the field at sunrise. I do not recollect ever seeing my mother by the light of day."
3. Young Frederick became determined to read and write. He traded bread with white boys for reading lessons. But when he was sent away to a cruel new master, he was beaten with a whip until he was bloody and scarred. He was not given enough to eat. He was sent into the fields to work long, long hours. He saw the terrible things that happen when one person has complete control over another. He says, "But for the hope of being free, I have no doubt that I should have killed myself."
4. What happened next is all put down in a book he wrote called *Narrative of the Life of Frederick Douglass, An American Slave*. But he didn't tell how he escaped to freedom. If he had, the slave catchers would have known how to capture others who were using the same route. Frederick Douglass kept telling people this simple truth: "Justice to the Negro is safety to the nation." And he said things like this: "People in general will say they like colored men as well as any other, but in their proper place. They assign us that place; they don't let us do it ourselves nor will they allow us a voice in the decision. They will not allow that we have a head to think, and a heart to feel and a soul to aspire. You **degrade** us, and then ask why we are degraded—you shut our mouths and then ask why we don't speak—you close your colleges and **seminaries** against us, and then ask why we don't know more."

Definitions

Degrade: to treat someone without respect

Seminaries: colleges for training priests and ministers

EXPEDITIONARY LEARNING

Mid-Unit Assessment

Using Evidence to Support Analysis

"Frederick Douglass"

Name: Darion Bell

Date: Jan 13, 2018

Directions: Read the "Frederick Douglass" text and then answer the following questions.

1. How did slavery affect Douglass's relationship with his mother? Support your answer with evidence from the text.

he never saw his mother more than four or five times in his life.

2. All of the following are evidence that Douglass's master was cruel except
   a. He traded bread with white boys for reading lessons.
   b. He was beaten with a whip until he was bloody and scarred.
   c. He was not given enough to eat.
   d. He was sent into the fields to work long, long hours.

3. What argument is Douglass making when he says, "You close your colleges and seminaries against us, and then ask why we don't know more"? Support your answer with evidence from the text.

You degrade us, and then ask why we are degraded - you shut our mouths and then ask why we don't speak you close your colleges and seminaries against us.

EXPEDITIONARY LEARNING

4. Which of the following conclusions about Douglass does the text provide strong evidence for?

   a. Douglass inspired many people to join the abolition movement.

   b. Douglass never overcame his sense of inferiority because he had been a slave.

   c. Douglass was very courageous.

   d. Douglass hated the United States because it allowed slavery.

   Explain your answer in a well-written paragraph that uses specific evidence from the text.

Douglass had did seminaries colleges for traning priests and ministers to treat someone with respect.

EXPEDITIONARY
LEARNING

Short Response 2-Point Holistic Rubric

Based on a rubric created for the New York State Common Core Curriculum.

The features of a **2-point response** are:

- Valid inferences and/or claims from the text where required by the prompt
- Evidence of analysis of the text where required by the prompt
- Relevant facts, definitions, concrete details, and/or other information from the text to develop a response according to the requirements of the prompt
- Sufficient number of facts, definitions, concrete details, and/or other information from the text as required by the prompt
- Complete sentences in which errors do not affect readability

The features of a **1-point response** are:

- A mostly literal recounting of events or details from the text as required by the prompt
- Some relevant facts, definitions, concrete details, and/or other information from the text to develop a response according to the requirements of the prompt
- Incomplete sentences or bullets

The features of a **0-point response** are:

- A response that does not address any of the requirements of the prompt or is totally inaccurate
- No response (blank answer)
- A response that is not written in English
- A response that is unintelligible or indecipherable

If the prompt requires two texts and the student references only one text, the response can be scored no higher than a 1.

EXPEDITIONARY LEARNING

"Renaissance Man" by Scott Kirkwood

Source: Kirkwood, Scott. "Renaissance Man." National Parks 87, *no. 2 (Spring 2013): 62.*

Name: Darion Bell

Date: Jan 18, 2018

Frederick Douglass's home tells the story of a man who overcame enormous obstacles and paved the way for others to do the same.

1. Take the Green Line subway train to Anacostia, Washington, D.C., and you'll find a house high on a hilltop. The man who lived in this house started a civil-rights movement long before MLK had landmarks named after him, long before the term "civil rights" even existed.
2. Walk into the visitor center at Frederick Douglass National Historic Site, and you'll hear a park volunteer repeat the words highlighted in the park's short film: "Agitate. Agitate. Agitate," she says. Agitate means to move things around, to stir the pot. That's what Frederick Douglass did. And he encouraged others to follow his lead.
3. Frederick Bailey was born a slave on a farm outside Easton, Maryland, in 1818. (After escaping from slavery in 1838, he would change his name to Douglass, to avoid being recaptured.) When he was only 8 years old, his slave master's wife taught him to read, using the Bible. When she was forced to stop, a young Douglass tricked other children into teaching him one letter of the alphabet at a time. "Words were the lever that Douglass used to change the world," says Braden Paynter, an interpretive ranger at the park.
4. As visitors entered the home, they were taken into the sitting room, where Douglass would teach his grandchildren history lessons. Beyond the living room is the study, where he would spend time reading one of the thousands of books he owned or drafting speeches and letters to friends, including Susan B. Anthony and Ida B. Wells.
5. How did Douglass rise from a slave to one of Washington's elite? When he was 20 years old, he borrowed papers from a free black sailor to escape from slavery, moving to New York, then New Bedford, Massachusetts. He soon helped William Lloyd Garrison and other key people in the abolitionist movement, who urged him to share his own experiences. Douglass's speeches became a powerful tool in the battle against slavery. Douglass was such a skilled speaker that some people began to doubt he was a fugitive (runaway) slave. To prove them wrong, he wrote his first autobiography in 1845, *Narrative of the Life of Frederick Douglass.* The narrative made him more well known, and put his freedom at risk once again.
6. To avoid being recaptured, Douglass fled to England. There, supporters purchased his freedom from his owners for $711. Douglass returned to the U.S. a free man and settled in Rochester, New York, the center of the abolitionist movement. Soon Douglass began using tactics that would gain popularity in the civil rights movement. In the early 1840s, he staged a sit-in on a segregated train car in Massachusetts. Prior to the Civil War in 1857, the Supreme Court ruled that fugitive slaves

could be captured in a free state, returned, and enslaved again. At this time Douglass thought about leaving the country for good.

7. But, eventually, he saw the Civil War as necessary to rid the country of slavery. Douglass even persuaded President Lincoln of the importance of ending slavery. After the Civil War ended and slavery was abolished, Douglass moved to Washington, D.C., where he would serve as the U.S. Marshal for the District of Columbia and the District's Recorder of Deeds.

8. Douglass died on February 20, 1895, at the age of 77. But his words live on as a testament to his work: "If there is no struggle, there is no progress. Those who favor freedom and yet deprecate [criticize] agitation, are men who want crops without plowing up the ground. They want the ocean without the awful roar of its many waters. Power concedes nothing without a demand. It never did and it never will."

EXPEDITIONARY
LEARNING

Text-Dependent Questions

"Renaissance Man"

Name: Darion Bell

Date: Jan 13/2018

Questions	Answers
Paragraph 2 What word is used to describe Frederick Douglass and why?	Frederick Douglass National historic Site
Paragraphs 3–5 Why are words so important to Frederick Douglass? Give at least two specific examples.	
Paragraphs 5–6 What are two ways that Frederick Douglass gets his freedom?	
Paragraph 8 Frederick Douglass said, "If there is no struggle, there is no progress. Those who favor freedom and yet deprecate [criticize] agitation, are men who want crops without plowing up the ground. They want the ocean without the awful roar of its many waters. Power concedes nothing without a demand. It never did and it never will." What does he mean by this quote, and how do you know?	

EXPEDITIONARY LEARNING

Entry Task

Frederick Douglass Timeline

Name: Darion Bell

Date:

1818 Frederick Douglass was born a slave in Tuckahoe, Maryland.

As a child/teen Frederick Douglass learned to read and write. 1824

1838 Douglass escaped and went to New York City, then settled in New Bedford, Connecticut.

1841 Douglass became involved with the abolition movement and worked as speaker, traveling all over the country and making speeches in favor of abolition.

1845 wrote the narrtive of the life of fredrick douglass

1845–1847 Douglass traveled in England and Ireland.

1847 Douglass returned to the United States and settled in Rochester, New York. He published an abolitionist newspaper and worked for equality for African Americans and women.

1861–1865 U.S. Civil War: Douglass advocated for African American soldiers to be allowed to fight with the Union Army and helped recruit for the first black regiment: the Massachusetts 54th.

1865 Thirteenth Amendment ended slavery.

1872 Douglass moved to Washington, D.C. He held a number of positions, including federal marshal and envoy to Haiti.

1895 Douglass died; he was buried in Mount Hope Cemetery in Rochester, New York.

1. On the timeline, add the event "Wrote *Narrative of the Life of Frederick Douglass*" in the correct location.
2. Choose one important event from Douglass's life that happened *before* he wrote the *Narrative*. Explain that event and why it was important.

1838 met and fell in love with Anna murray a free black woman in Baltimore marriage lasted 44yrs

3. Choose one important event from Douglass's life that happened *after* he wrote the *Narrative.* Explain that event and why it was important.

EXPEDITIONARY LEARNING

Douglass's Homes Discussion Appointments

Name: Darion Bell

Date: Jan 15, 2018

Directions: Make one appointment at each location.

In Tuckahoe, Maryland: Nyla

In Baltimore, Maryland: Terrell

In Rochester, New York: Cekeria

In Washington, D.C.: Garrott Bagwell

EXPEDITIONARY
LEARNING

Text and Questions

Frederick Douglass's Purpose

Source: Douglass, Frederick. Narrative of the Life of Frederick Douglass. *Boston, Massachusetts: Anti-Slavery Office, 1845. Project Gutenberg. http://www.gutenberg.org/files/23/23-h/23-h.htm.*

90

Name: Darion Bell

Date: Jan 15, 2018

The quote below is how Frederick Douglass ends the *Narrative*	Questions
Sincerely and earnestly hoping that this little book may do something toward throwing light on the American slave system, and **hastening** the glad day of deliverance to the millions of my brethren in bonds—faithfully relying on the power of truth, love and justice, for success in my humble efforts—and solemnly pledging my self anew to the sacred cause, I **subscribe myself**, Frederick Douglass.	**Answer these questions as you read. Also, write the definitions of new words here.** 1. What does it mean to "throw light on" something? give it some atteion.
	Hastening: to make arrive more quickly 2. What does "the glad day of deliverance" mean in this sentence? Your giving somebody something.
	Subscribe myself: write my name 3. What is "the sacred cause"? freedom
	Answer this question after you have read the whole quote. 4. What is Frederick Douglass's purpose? he wants to stop slavery.

EXPEDITIONARY LEARNING

Shining a Light Anchor Chart

Name: Darion

Date: Jan 15, 2018

	People who defend slavery may think . . .	Frederick Douglass's position
How slavery affects slaves	Slaver isn't that bad	terrible for slaves
How slavery affects slave owners	slaver is good for slaver owners.	courpted slave owners.
The effects of the institution of slavery	they may think that they are getting inspired and more treating and they are not getting disrespet	he wants slavery to stop and he want them to be who they are and he wants everbody to no that they are just pople.

EXPEDITIONARY LEARNING

Position Cards

Slavery isn't that bad for slaves. In fact, they are mostly content with their lot. they are not happy geting hurt and stressed	**Slavery is terrible for slaves.** becaus they are Getting hurt.	**The institution of slavery is necessary.** • It reflects the natural racial order. • Slavery brings the civilizing influence of Christianity to Africans, who would otherwise be uncivilized and immoral. • Slavery creates an orderly society.
Slavery is good for slave owners. its not because they are being forced.	**Slavery corrupts slaveholders.** So they won't run away.	**The institution of slavery is abhorrent, and the arguments people make about its importance in creating a well-ordered and civilized society are incorrect.**

EXPEDITIONARY
LEARNING

Determining Position

Name: Darion Bell

Date: Jan 16, 2018

Directions: Read each quote. Then decide which box the quote would go in on the Shining a Light Anchor Chart. Write down the number of that box and explain your reasoning in the space provided.

	People who defend slavery may think . . .	Frederick Douglass's position
How slavery affects slaves	1 They are using People	2 Frederick douglass's don't like slavery
How slavery affects slave owners	3 They do not obey them;	4 Slavery is terrible for Slaves.
The effects of the institution of slavery	5 Slavery corrupts,	6 The insititution of slavery is abhorrent.

Directions: Read each quote. Then decide which box the quote would go in on the Shining a Light Anchor Chart. Write down the number of that box and explain your reasoning in the space provided.

Quote	Into which box of the Shining a Light Anchor Chart would this quote best fit?	Why does this quote match the position you have chosen?
"The [slave] children unable to work in the field had neither shoes, stockings, jackets, nor trousers, given to them; their clothing consisted of two coarse linen shirts per year. When these failed them, they went naked until the next allowance-day."	They had to sleep on the ground because they did not want to waste money on them.	
"Singing, among slaves, [is] evidence of their contentment and happiness."	the only happiness is that they can fly.	
"He was a cruel man, hardened by a long life of slave-holding."	that is the slave master	
The songs sung by slaves "told a tale of woe . . . they breathed the prayer and complaint of souls boiling over with the bitterest anguish."	it was the little kids singing a song in the forest	

EXPEDITIONARY LEARNING

Entry Task

Quote Cards

"The [slave] children unable to work in the field had neither shoes, stockings, jackets, nor trousers, given to them; their clothing consisted of two coarse linen shirts per year. When these failed them, they went naked until the next allowance-day."

"Singing, among slaves, [is] evidence of their contentment and happiness."

"He was a cruel man, hardened by a long life of slave-holding."

The songs sung by slaves "told a tale of woe . . . they breathed the prayer and complaint of souls boiling over with the bitterest anguish."

EXPEDITIONARY LEARNING

Text and Questions (Excerpt 1)

Narrative of the Life of Frederick Douglass

Source: Douglass, Frederick. Narrative of the Life of Frederick Douglass. *Boston, Massachusetts: Anti-Slavery Office, 1845. Project Gutenberg. http://www.gutenberg.org/files/23/23-h/23-h.htm.*

Name: Darion Bell

Date: Jan 16, 2018

Chapter 1, Paragraphs 1–5 and 8

Text	Second Read Questions	Third Read Questions
1. I was born in Tuckahoe, near Hillsborough, and about twelve miles from Easton, in Talbot county, Maryland. I have no accurate knowledge of my age, never having seen any authentic record containing it. By far the larger part of the slaves know as little of their ages as horses know of theirs, and it is the wish of most masters within my knowledge to keep their slaves thus **ignorant**. I do not remember to have ever met a slave who could tell of his birthday. They **seldom** come nearer to it than planting-time, harvest-time, cherry-time, spring-time, or fall-time. A want of information concerning my own was a source of unhappiness to me even	1. What do slaves not have knowledge about? 2. Who prevents slaves from having this knowledge? **Ignorant:** not knowing facts you should know **Seldom:** not often 1. age and birthdays The slave know as little of their ages, 2. master	1. Frederick Douglass begins his story with an example of how slaves are mistreated. What example does he give? By far the larger part of slaves know as little of their ages as horses know of theirs, and it is the wish of most masters within my knowledge to keep their slaves thus ignorant.

during childhood. The white children could tell their ages. I could not tell why I ought to be **deprived** of the same **privilege**. I was not allowed to make any **inquiries** of my master concerning it. He deemed all such **inquiries** on the part of a slave **improper** and **impertinent**, and evidence of a restless spirit. The nearest estimate I can give makes me now between twenty-seven and twenty-eight years of age. I come to this, from hearing my master say, some time during 1835, I was about seventeen years old.	**Deprived:** **Privilege:** 3. The root of inquiries is *quir-*, meaning seek/ask. Based on this, what does the word *inquiries* mean? **Improper:** wrong **Impertinent:** rude and disrespectful Inquiries - asking for information.	deprived - suffering a severe and damaging lack of basic material and cultural benefits. Privilege - a speciel right, advantage, or immunity granted or available only to a particular person or group.
2. My mother was named Harriet Bailey. She was the daughter of Isaac and Betsey Bailey, both colored, and quite dark. My mother was of a darker complexion than either my grandmother or grandfather.	She takes care of the slaver babes caus they don't want them runing araund,	
3. My father was a white man. He was admitted to be such by all I ever heard speak of my parentage. The opinion was also whispered that my master was my father; but of the correctness of this opinion, I know nothing; the means of knowing was withheld from me. My mother and I were separated when I was but	4. Who was Frederick Douglass's father? 5. Paraphrase this sentence in your own words: "He was admitted to be such by all I ever heard speak of my parentage." My father was a white man. He was also my mas	2. This paragraph discusses Douglass's parents. What does it show about how slavery affected children's relationships with their parents? by destroying the relationships. A negative affect on the bonds between the parents and child were not valued and to destroy the natural affection of the mother for her child.

an infant—before I knew her as my mother. It is a common custom, in the part of Maryland from which I ran away, to part children from their mothers at a very early age. Frequently, before the child has reached its twelfth month, its mother is taken from it, and hired out on some farm a considerable distance off, and the child is placed under the care of an old woman, too old for field **labor**. For what this separation is done, I do not know, unless it be to **hinder** the development of the child's affection toward its mother, and to **blunt** and destroy the natural affection of the mother for the child. This is the **inevitable** result.	**Labor:** work **Hinder:** **Blunt:** worn down, less sharp **Inevitable:** certain to happen	3. What do these words mean: "to blunt and destroy the natural affection of the mother for the child"? How do they add to the overall point of the paragraph? to blunt and destroy the natural affection of the mother child means to make it weaker over time. This words add to the paragraph by cause they want them to see what happens.
4. I never saw my mother, to know her as such, more than four or five times in my life; and each of these times was very short in **duration**, and at night. She was hired by a Mr. Stewart, who lived about twelve miles from my home. She made her journeys to see me in the night, travelling the whole distance on foot, after the performance of her day's work. She was a field hand, and a whipping is the **penalty** of not being in the field at sunrise, unless a	**Duration:** **Penalty:** punishment	4. How does this information about Douglass's mother connect to what you learned in articles you read about Frederick Douglass in Lesson 5?

slave has special permission from his or her master to the contrary—a permission which they **seldom** get, and one that gives to him that gives it the proud name of being a kind master. I do not recollect of ever seeing my mother by the light of day. She was with me in the night. She would lie down with me, and get me to sleep, but long before I waked she was gone. Very little communication ever took place between us. Death soon ended what little we could have while she lived, and with it her **hardships** and suffering. She died when I was about seven years old, on one of my master's farms, near Lee's Mill. I was not allowed to be present during her illness, at her death, or burial. She was gone long before I knew any thing about it. Never having enjoyed, to any considerable extent, her soothing presence, her tender and watchful care, I received the **tidings** of her death with much the same emotions I should have probably felt at the death of a stranger.	**Seldom:** not often **Hardships:** **Tidings:** news 6. What was Frederick Douglass's relationship with his mother like? It was bad 7. Paraphrase this sentence: "Never having enjoyed, to any considerable extent, her soothing presence, her tender and watchful care, I received the tidings of her death with much the same emotions I should have probably felt at the death of a stranger."	

5. Called thus suddenly away, she [my mother] left me without the slightest **intimation** of who my father was. The whisper that my master was my father, may or may not be true; and, true or false, it is of but little consequence to my purpose whilst the fact remains, in all its glaring **odiousness**, that slaveholders have **ordained**, and by law established, that the children of slave women shall in all cases follow the **condition** of their mothers; and this is done too obviously to **administer to their own lusts**, and make a **gratification** of their wicked desires profitable as well as pleasurable; for by this **cunning** arrangement, the slaveholder, in cases not a few, **sustains** to his slaves the double relation of master and father.	**Intimation:** hint 8. Who did people think Douglass's father was? 9. The suffix of *odiousness* is *-ness*. What does *-ness* mean? Based on the meaning of the suffix *-ness*, what does *odiousness* mean? **Ordained:** ordered **Condition:** **Administer to their own lusts:** take care of their own (sexual) desires **Cunning:** clever **Sustains:** to make something continue to exist 10. Are the children of slave mothers free or slaves? 11. The root of gratification is *grat-*. What does *grat-* mean? Based on the root *grat*, what does the word *gratification* mean?	
6. I have had two masters. My first master's name was Anthony. I do not remember his first name. He was generally called Captain Anthony—a title which, I presume, he acquired by sailing a craft on the Chesapeake Bay.		5. How does having power over their slaves seem to affect the overseer and the owner? 6. What scene does Douglass vividly describe? Why do you think he describes it in such detail? How does this serve his purpose?

He was not considered a rich slaveholder. He owned two or three farms, and about thirty slaves. His farms and slaves were under the care of an overseer. The overseer's name was Plummer. Mr. Plummer was a miserable drunkard, a profane swearer, and a savage monster. He always went armed with a **cowskin** and a heavy cudgel. I have known him to cut and slash the women's heads so horribly, that even master would be enraged at his cruelty, and would threaten to whip him if he did not mind himself. Master, however, was not a **humane** slaveholder. It required extraordinary **barbarity** on the part of an overseer to affect him. He was a cruel man, **hardened** by a long life of slaveholding. He would at times seem to take great pleasure in whipping a slave. I have often been awakened at the dawn of day by the most heart-rending shrieks of an own aunt of mine, whom he used to tie up to a **joist**, and whip upon her naked back till she was literally covered	**Cowskin:** a whip made of leather **Humane:** treating people in a way that does not cause suffering **Barbarity:** cruelty **Hardened:** 12. Who was cruel? 13. Who is being whipped? **Joist:** beam that supports the roof (in a house)	

with blood. No words, no tears, no prayers, from his **gory** victim, seemed to move his iron heart from its bloody purpose. The louder she screamed, the harder he whipped; and where the blood ran fastest, there he whipped longest. He would whip her to make her scream, and whip her to make her hush; and not until overcome by fatigue, would he cease to swing the blood-clotted cowskin. I remember the first time I ever witnessed this horrible exhibition. I was quite a child, but I well remember it. I never shall forget it whilst I remember any thing. It was the first of a long series of such outrages, of which I was doomed to be a witness and a participant. It struck me with awful force. It was the blood-stained gate, the entrance to the hell of slavery, through which I was about to pass. It was a most terrible **spectacle**. I wish I could commit to paper the feelings with which I beheld it.	**Gory:** 14. Rewrite the following sentence in your own words: "No words, no tears, no prayers, from his gory victim, seemed to move his iron heart from its bloody purpose." **Spectacle:** he is trying to end slavery cause he don't like what the slave master is doing to them and he wants to stop it so that they won't get hurt any more.	

Whole Excerpt PURPOSE: How does this excerpt support the two positions Douglass held about slavery that are listed below?

1. Slavery is terrible for slaves.

cause they are using People for there being.

2. Slavery corrupts slaveholders.

They are using them for drugs and Sugar.

EXPEDITIONARY LEARNING

Reference Sheet

Roots, Prefixes, and Suffixes

Name: Darion Bell

Date: Jan 18, 2018

Directions: Words from *Narrative Life of Frederick Douglass* that contain common roots, prefixes, and suffixes are recorded below. Use this reference sheet to assist you in determining the meaning of words.

Common Roots (base)	Meaning	Example (excerpt number, if applicable)
sol/sole	One, only, alone	Desolate by there self
pos	From *positus*: placed	Disposition (4) get in order.
quir	Seek, ask	Inquiries (1) queistions
grat	Pleasing	Gratification (1) matarica

Common Prefixes (beginning)	Meaning	Example (excerpt number, if applicable)
de-	Away from, without	Deprived (1), desolate, devoted
re-	Again or back	Reduced (3), revived (4), rekindle (4), recounted (5)
dis-	Take away	Discontentment (3), disposition (4)

Common Suffixes (end)	Meaning	Example (excerpt number, if applicable)
-able	Capable of	Miserable (1), unmanageable, valuable (3), liable (5)
-ness	State of	Odiousness (1)
-ful	Full of	Needful

EXPEDITIONARY
LEARNING

Entry Task

Roots, Prefixes, and Suffixes

Name: ______________________________

Date: ______________________________

Directions: Identify the meaning of the root, prefix, or suffix in the underlined word using your Reference Sheet: Roots, Prefixes, and Suffixes. Then determine the meaning of the entire word.

Sentence from *Narrative of the Life of Frederick Douglass*	Meaning of Root/Prefix/ Suffix	Meaning of Underlined Word
I was somewhat unmanageable when I first went there, but a few months of this discipline tamed me.	*un*: not *able*:	
My natural elasticity was crushed, my intellect languished, the disposition to read departed, the cheerful spark that lingered about my eye died; the dark night of slavery closed in upon me; and behold a man transformed into a brute!	*dis*:	
His life was devoted to planning and perpetrating the grossest deceptions.	*de*:	

EXPEDITIONARY LEARNING

Constructed Response (Excerpt 1)

Name: Darion Bell

Date: Jan 23, 2018

Directions: Reread Excerpt 1 from *Narrative of the Life of Frederick Douglass*. In a one-paragraph response, answer the question "What two things was Douglass deprived of as a child that his audience thinks every child should have?" Remember to recycle the prompt, use textual evidence to support your ideas, and write in complete sentences.

Deprived: not having things that are necessary.

(1) Frederick Douglass – he never knew his father and only seen his mother a handful of times before she dies – and then, he isn't allowed to go to her funeral.

(2) Every child deserves loving parents, education and freedom.

Text and Questions (Excerpt 2)

Narrative of the Life of Frederick Douglass

Source: Douglass, Frederick. Narrative of the Life of Frederick Douglass. *Boston, Massachusetts: Anti-Slavery Office, 1845. Project Gutenberg. http://www.gutenberg.org/files/23/23-h/23-h.htm.*

Name: Darion Bell

Date: Jan 18, 2019

Chapter 2, Paragraphs 2–5, (7–8), 10–11

Text	Second Read Questions	Third Read Questions
1. Colonel Lloyd kept from three to four hundred slaves on his home plantation [called Great House Farm], and owned a large number more on the neighboring farms belonging to him. This [Great House Farm] was the great business place. It was the **seat of government** for the whole twenty farms.	**Seat of government:** Great house farm	why did they need slaves to do there work.
2. Here, too, the slaves of all the other farms received their monthly **allowance** of food, and their yearly clothing. The men and women slaves received, as their monthly allowance of food, eight pounds of pork, or its equivalent in fish, and one **bushel** of corn meal. Their yearly clothing consisted of two **coarse** linen shirts, one pair of linen trousers, like the shirts, one jacket, one pair of trousers for winter, made of coarse negro cloth, one pair of stockings, and one pair of shoes; the whole of which could not have cost more than seven dollars. The allowance of the slave children was given to their mothers, or the old women having the care of them.	**Allowance:** a set amount provided to someone, often of food **Bushel:** a measure of about 8 gallons **Coarse:** rough, not soft 1. How many pairs of pants did adult slaves have? 2 pair of pants 2. Why were many children naked? not enough money.	1. Why does Douglass describe the clothing that slaves were given in such detail? What is he trying to show?

The children unable to work in the field had neither shoes, stockings, jackets, nor trousers, given to them; their clothing consisted of two coarse linen shirts per year. When these failed them, they went naked until the next allowance-day. Children from seven to ten years old, of both sexes, almost naked, might be seen at all seasons of the year.		
3. There were no beds given the slaves, unless one coarse blanket be considered such, and none but the men and women had these. This, however, is not considered a very great **privation**. They find less difficulty from the **want** of beds, than from the **want** of time to sleep; for when their day's work in the field is done, the most of them having their washing, mending, and cooking to do, and having few or none of the ordinary **facilities** for doing either of these, very many of their sleeping hours are **consumed** in preparing for the field the coming day; and when this is done, old and young, male and female, married and single, drop down side by side, on one common bed, —the cold, damp floor,—each covering himself or herself with their miserable blankets; and here they sleep till they are **summoned** to the field by the **driver's** horn. At the sound of this, all must rise, and be off to the field. There must be no halting; every one must be at his or her **post**; and **woe betides them** who hear not this morning **summons** to the field; for if they are not awakened by the sense of hearing, they are by the sense of feeling: no age nor sex finds any favor. Mr. Severe, the overseer, used to stand by the door of the **quarter**, armed with a large hickory stick and heavy cowskin, ready to whip any one who was so unfortunate as not to hear, or, from any other cause, was prevented from being ready to start for the field at the sound of the horn.	**Privation:** a lack of something necessary for survival **Want:** **Facilities:** spaces, equipment **Consumed:** 3. Where do slaves sleep? **Summoned:** **Driver:** a person who supervised slaves as they worked; often, a plantation would have an overseer and then several drivers who reported to the overseer **Post:** the place where you do your job **Woe betides them:** **Summons:** **Quarter:** the place where slaves lived 4. What happened to slaves who did not get to the field on time?	2. Why didn't slaves get enough sleep?

EXPEDITIONARY LEARNING

4. Mr. Severe was rightly named: he was a cruel man. I have seen him whip a woman, causing the blood to run half an hour at the time; and this, too, in the midst of her crying children, pleading for their mother's release. He seemed to take pleasure in manifesting his **fiendish barbarity**. Added to his cruelty, he was a **profane** swearer. It was enough to chill the blood and stiffen the hair of an ordinary man to hear him talk. Scarce a sentence escaped him but that was **commenced** or concluded by some horrid oath. The field was the place to witness his cruelty and **profanity**. His presence made it both the field of blood and of **blasphemy**. From the rising till the going down of the sun, he was cursing, raving, cutting, and slashing among the slaves of the field, in the most frightful manner. His career was short. He died very soon after I went to Colonel Lloyd's; and he died as he lived, uttering, with his dying groans, bitter curses and horrid oaths. His death was regarded by the slaves as the result of a **merciful providence**.	**Fiendish barbarity:** unpleasant cruelties **Profane:** **Commenced:** **Profanity:** **Blasphemy:** something you say or do that is insulting to God or people's religious beliefs 5. Paraphrase the sentence "His presence made it both the field of blood and of blasphemy." 6. What was Mr. Severe like? **Merciful providence:** a force that is meant to protect us	(5) reverberate with their wild songs revealing at once the highest joy and the deepest sadness. (6) he was a crule man. I have seen him whip a woman causing the
5. The home plantation of Colonel Lloyd **wore the appearance** of a country village. . . . It was called by the slaves the *Great House Farm.* The slaves selected to go to the Great House Farm, for the monthly allowance for themselves and their fellow-slaves, were peculiarly enthusiastic. While on their way, they would make the dense old woods, for miles around, **reverberate** with their wild songs, revealing at once the highest joy and the deepest sadness. They would compose and sing as they went along, consulting neither time nor tune.	**Wore the appearance of:** **Reverberate:** echo 7. What do the slaves do as they walk to the Great House Farm? They sing in the dark while they are going to the house farm	

6. I did not, when a slave, understand the deep meaning of those rude and apparently **incoherent** songs. I was myself within the circle; so that I neither saw nor heard as those without might see and hear. They told a tale of **woe** which was then altogether beyond my feeble comprehension; they were tones loud, long, and deep; they breathed the prayer and complaint of souls boiling over with the bitterest **anguish**. Every tone was a testimony against slavery, and a prayer to God for deliverance from chains. The hearing of those wild notes always depressed my spirit, and filled me with **ineffable** sadness. I have frequently found myself in tears while hearing them. The mere recurrence to those songs, even now, **afflicts** me; and while I am writing these lines, an expression of feeling has already found its way down my cheek. To those songs I trace my first glimmering **conception** of the **dehumanizing** character of slavery. I can never get rid of that conception. Those songs still follow me, to deepen my hatred of slavery, and **quicken** my sympathies for my **brethren** in bonds. If any one wishes to be impressed with the soul-killing effects of slavery, let him go to Colonel Lloyd's plantation, and, on allowance-day, place himself in the deep pine woods, and there let him, in silence, analyze the sounds that shall pass through the chambers of his soul,—and if he is not thus impressed, it will only be because "there is no flesh in his **obdurate** heart."	**Incoherent:** 8. To what does "they" in the third sentence refer? **Woe:** sorrow **Anguish:** 9. How did Douglass feel when he heard the slaves singing? **Ineffable:** too great to be described in words **Afflicts:** **Conception:** **Dehumanizing:** treating people so badly that they lose their good human qualities **Quicken:** to make grow **Brethren:** member of a group **Obdurate:** stubborn, hard 10. If someone listens to the songs and is not moved by them, what does Douglass suggest that person is missing?	3. What emotions did Douglass say that the songs sung by slaves conveyed? 4. Why does Douglass explain that even thinking about the songs now makes him sad? How does that help convince his audience?

every tone was a testimony against.

i read that they are not happy and they are not getting money.

7. I have often been utterly **astonished**, since I came to the north, to find persons who could speak of the singing, among slaves, as evidence of their contentment and happiness. It is impossible to **conceive** of a greater mistake. Slaves sing most when they are most unhappy. The songs of the slave represent the sorrows of his heart; and he is relieved by them, only as an aching heart is relieved by its tears. At least, such is my experience. I have often sung to drown my sorrow, but seldom to express my happiness. Crying for joy, and singing for joy, were alike uncommon to me while in the jaws of slavery. The singing of a man cast away upon a **desolate** island might be as appropriately considered as evidence of contentment and happiness, as the singing of a slave; the songs of the one and of the other are **prompted** by the same emotion.	**Astonished:** very surprised **Conceive:** 11. What root and prefix is the word *desolate* made up of? Based on the meanings of those word roots, what do you think the word *desolate* means? **Prompted:** 12. Does happiness or sorrow prompt slaves to sing?	

Whole Excerpt

PURPOSE: How does this excerpt support the two positions Douglass held about slavery that are listed below?

1. Slavery is terrible for slaves.

2. Slavery corrupts slaveholders.

Sentence/Paraphrase Cards (Excerpt 2)

SENTENCE	PARAPHRASE
Their yearly clothing consisted of two coarse linen shirts, one pair of linen trousers, like the shirts, one jacket, one pair of trousers for winter, made of coarse negro cloth, one pair of stockings, and one pair of shoes; the whole of which could not have cost more than seven dollars.	Every year, a slave was given two rough linen shirts, one pair of pants, one jacket, one pair of winter pants, one pair of socks, and one pair of shoes. All of these together cost less than seven dollars.
SENTENCE	**PARAPHRASE**
The children unable to work in the field had neither shoes, stockings, jackets, nor trousers, given to them; their clothing consisted of two coarse linen shirts per year.	Children who were not old enough to work in the fields did not get shoes, socks, jacket, or pants. They got only two shirts per year.
SENTENCE	**PARAPHRASE**
They find less difficulty from the want of beds, than from the want of time to sleep; for when their day's work in the field is done, the most of them having their washing, mending, and cooking to do, and having few or none of the ordinary facilities for doing either of these, very many of their sleeping hours are consumed in preparing for the field the coming day.	The biggest difficulty for slaves is not that they don't have beds, but that they don't have time to sleep. When they are done working in the field, they have to do the regular household chores like washing and mending, but they don't have good equipment to do them. As a result, they have to spend a lot of the night getting their chores done to be ready to work in the field again the next day.
SENTENCE	**PARAPHRASE**
Mr. Severe, the overseer, used to stand by the door of the quarter, armed with a large hickory stick and heavy cowskin, ready to whip any one who was so unfortunate as not to hear, or, from any other cause, was prevented from being ready to start for the field at the sound of the horn.	Mr. Severe, the overseer, held a whip and a stick, and stood near where the slaves lived. He was ready to whip anyone who did not hear the horn or who for any reason was not ready to start walking to the field on time.

SENTENCE	PARAPHRASE
The mere recurrence to those songs, even now, afflicts me; and while I am writing these lines, an expression of feeling has already found its way down my cheek.	Even thinking of these songs makes me sad. While I am writing, a tear has rolled down my cheek.
SENTENCE	**PARAPHRASE**
The singing of a man cast away upon a desolate island might be as appropriately considered as evidence of contentment and happiness, as the singing of a slave; the song of the one and of the other are prompted by the same emotion.	It is inappropriate to think that a man who is stranded on a desert island and is singing is happy. It is just as inappropriate to think that a slave who is singing is happy. They are both singing to express the same emotion.

Entry Task

Powerful Stories

Directions: Skim Excerpt 1 and Excerpt 2 from the *Narrative*. Put a star next to a sentence that you found particularly powerful.

EXPEDITIONARY
LEARNING

Analysis Note-Catcher (Excerpt 2)

Narrative of the Life of Frederick Douglass

Name: Darion Bell

Date: Jan 1/25, 2019

Chapter 2, Paragraphs 2–5, (7–8), and 10–11

What does Douglass say? What is this excerpt about?	*Living conditions for slaves are terrible, and overseers like Mr. Severe treat them very badly. Slaves express their sorrow by singing. People in the North think that the singing is showing slaves' contentment with their lot, but that is not true.*	
Position: Why does he say it? Briefly explain the connection between this excerpt and each of the following positions.	**Evidence: What words, phrases, and sentences show his position?** (Choose 1 or 2 quotes for each position; give the source and briefly state what each refers to.)	**Analysis: What is the position that Douglass is trying to disprove? How does this quote prove that this position is incorrect?**
Slavery corrupts slave owners. **Slavery was terrible for slaves.**	They have no beds to sleep on and they sleep on the floor and they are having kids and they have to put them in a shelter when a lady takes care of them.	he is trying to disprove slavey cause they are hurting inside and outside cause they are forced to work

EXPEDITIONARY LEARNING

Found Poem

Name: Darion Bell

Date: 1/25/2019 Jan

1. Carefully reread Excerpt 2 and look for 10–20 words or phrases that stand out about living and working conditions for slaves on plantations. Highlight or underline details, words, and phrases that you find particularly powerful, moving, or interesting.
2. On a separate sheet of paper, make a list of the details, words, and phrases you underlined, keeping them in the order in which you found them.
3. Look back over your list and cut out everything that is dull or unnecessary or that just doesn't seem right for a poem about what life was like for slaves on plantations. Your whole poem should be fewer than 30 words.
4. When you're close to an edited version, if you absolutely need to add a word or two to make the poem flow more smoothly, to make sense, to make a point, *you may add up to two words of your own*. That's two and only two!
5. Arrange the words so that they make a rhythm you like. You can space words out so that they are all alone or all run together. You can also put key words on lines by themselves.
6. Choose a title.

Model (about Douglass's mother; from Excerpt 1)

Mother in the night

Mother
<u>She journeyed to see me in the night</u>
<u>Lying</u> beside me
Never by the <u>light of day</u>
<u>Whipping—the penalty</u>
But worse yet,
Even in death,
She was a stranger
to me.

EXPEDITIONARY LEARNING

Found poem title: 5

Mother She Journeyed to See
in the night Lying beside me
Never by the light of day
whipping – the Penalty
But worse yet Even
in Death she was a Stranger
to me.

Entry Task

My Independent Reading Plan

Name: Darion Bell

Date: Jan 31, 2019

Title of book: Desti

Final project due: twomorraw

Number of pages: 1 days to read 15 = ______
(pages to read each day)

1. Why did you choose this book?

It was about Destinaton everest.

2. What is the setting (time and place) of this book?

It was in the cabin.

3. After reading the first couple of pages (or chapters), what is your impression of the characters? Why do you get that impression? Cite some textual evidence. (Use the back if necessary.)

they was on a plain going to the spot were toe climb the moutain.

4. What have you struggled with in past independent reading projects? What are three specific actions you will take that will help you be successful this time around? (Use the back if necessary.)

they have made it to the top and reach ther goal.

EXPEDITIONARY LEARNING

Quotes on Poetry by James Dickey

Source: http://www.brainpickings.org/index.php/2013/03/11/how-to-enjoy-poetry/.

"What is poetry? And why has it been around so long? . . . When you really feel it, a new part of you happens, or an old part is renewed, with surprise and delight at being what it is."

"Part of the spell of poetry is the rhythm of language, used by poets who understand how powerful a factor rhythm can be, how compelling and unforgettable. Almost anything put into rhyme is more memorable than the same thing in prose. Why this is, no one knows completely, though the answer is surely rooted far down in the biology by means of which we exist; in the circulation of the blood that goes forth from the heart and comes back, and in the repetition of breathing."

Poet’s Toolbox Anchor Chart

Figurative Language	Sound	Form
Metaphor	Alliteration	Line length
Extended metaphor	Onomatopoeia	Poetic inversion
Simile	Repetition	
Personification	Assonance	
Allusion	Consonance	
Apostrophe	Rhyme scheme	
Vivid word choice		
Juxtaposition		

EXPEDITIONARY LEARNING

Poet's Toolbox Reference Sheet

Name: Darion Bell

Date: Jan 31/2019

	Definition	Function	Example
FIGURATIVE LANGUAGE	**What is it?**	**How does it contribute to meaning?**	**What does it look like?**
Metaphor	An implied comparison between two unlike things that have something important in common	Clarifies the qualities of the thing the author is comparing—for example, hope, like a bird, sings and gives happiness to a person	"'Hope' is the thing with feathers" (Emily Dickinson)
Extended metaphor	A metaphor that continues for several stanzas or the length of a poem	By using this device, the author can thoroughly examine the similarities between the two unlike things.	"The Fog" by Robert Frost is a short poem with an extended metaphor.
Simile	A comparison using *like* or *as* between two unlike things that have something important in common	Same as metaphor	"O my Love's like a red, red rose, / that's newly sprung in June" (Robert Burns)
Personification	A device through which inanimate objects are given human characteristics	Helps the reader understand the purpose or visualize the inanimate object. Heightens the importance of the object.	"The eyes of the old house / watch me as I pass by" (Sharon Ruebel)
Allusion	A device through which the speaker refers to something that the reader needs prior knowledge of or experience with in order to understand	It functions similarly to a metaphor. The reader can understand a complex concept quickly.	This sports team is a Cinderella story!

Apostrophe	A device through which the speaker talks directly to an absent person, living or dead, or even a nonexistent person or thing as if it were capable of understanding	Heightens the emotion of the poem	"Death, be not proud" (John Donne)
Vivid word choice	A device through which the author chooses nouns, adjectives, or verbs that paint a strong mental picture and often have layers of meaning	Helps the reader visualize the images	Instead of saying "The dogs are mean," the author says, "The dogs prowled, looking to attack."
Juxtaposition	The placing of two things that directly oppose each other (often abstract concepts) near each other or directly side by side so the reader can compare them	Helps the reader see the differences and similarities between the two things being juxtaposed and come to a deeper understanding of both	"A Long Walk to Water, or Love is like a soft cushion to sleep on while Hate is a stone."
SOUND	**What is it?**	**How does it contribute to meaning?**	**What does it look like?**
Alliteration	The repetition of beginning consonant sound	Creates rhythm, mood, and emphasizes the phrase	"doubting, dreaming dreams no mortals ever dared to dream before" (Edgar Allen Poe)
Onomatopoeia	Words that imitate the sound they are	Creates a strong mental image	*bark, buzz, squishy*
Repetition	When the author repeats something	Creates emphasis, rhythm, and mood	
Assonance	Repetition of internal vowels	Helps create rhyme, mood, and musicality in a poem	"the crumbling thunder of seas" (Robert Louis Stevenson)

Consonance	Repetition of ending (of the word or stressed syllable) consonant sound	Helps create rhythm and mood and emphasize a phrase	"Do not go gentle into that good night" (Dylan Thomas)
Rhyme scheme	The pattern of rhyme in a poem	Creates rhythmic, memorable language and makes the poem "sing." Also, when the pattern is broken, can create emphasis.	
FORM	**What is it?**	**How does it contribute to meaning?**	**What does it look like?**
Line length	The numbers of words in a line	Short lines can provide emphasis or give a choppy feel to the rhythm. Long lines can heighten emotion.	
Poetic inversion	A poet deliberately writes a sentence in a grammatically unusual way.	Catches the reader's attention, highlights the information in the line, or keeps the rhythm of the poem	"Like men we'll face the murderous, cowardly pack" (Claude McKay)

Lines from "If We Must Die" by Claude McKay

Source: McKay, Claude. "If We Must Die." Poetry.org. http://www.poets.org/viewmedia.php/prmMID/15250.

Being verbs: is are was were

While round us bark the mad and hungry dogs,

Making their mock at our accursèd lot.

Its tailking about
the dog are mocking

EXPEDITIONARY
LEARNING

Model Found Poem Draft 2

Mother

She journeyed to see me in the night
Immune to the weariness in her bones
While the moon illuminated her solitary walk.
Lying beside me
Like embers,
Like stones slowly baked by the sun,
Like the blanket she wished she could be.
Never by the light of day
Whipping—the penalty
But worse yet,
Even in death,
She was a stranger
to me.
That distance
Her feet couldn't cross.
Although led by her motherly heart,
she tried.
he felt happy that
he saw his mom
and that she hug
him.

EXPEDITIONARY
LEARNING

Entry Task

How to Read a Poem

Source: Collins, Billy. "Introduction to Poetry." Poetry 180: A Poem a Day for American High Schools. *Library of Congress. http://www.loc.gov/poetry/180/001.html.*

Name: Darion Bell

Date: Jan 2/5/2019

Directions: Please read the following poem and sketch three separate images you can picture in your mind as you read.

Introduction to Poetry

Billy Collins teacher

I ask them to take a poem
and hold it up to the light
like a color slide
or press an ear against its hive.
I say drop a mouse into a poem
and watch him probe his way out,
or walk inside the poem's room
and feel the walls for a light switch.
I want them to waterski
across the surface of a poem
waving at the author's name on the shore.
But all they want to do
is tie the poem to a chair with rope
and torture a confession out of it.
They begin beating it with a hose
to find out what it really means.

Image 1	Image 2	Image 3

EXPEDITIONARY
LEARNING

How to Read a Poem Anchor Chart

Focus: Poems use figurative language, sound, and form to create meaning.

Step 1: Paint Job Read

Read it aloud once.

What is the *title*? What does it have to do with the poem? different rivers

Who is the *speaker*? How do I know? names different rivers

What is the gist of the poem? What is the main idea of each *stanza* or section?

navin hues rivers

What is the overall feeling or *mood*? Does it change anywhere? singuler

What is my first impression of the *theme* (or statement or observation the poem is making about the world or the human condition)? singing

Step 2: Pop the Hood Read

Read it aloud again. While reading, underline anything that "pulls" you.

What words stick out to me? How do they contribute to the mood?

What poetic tools does the author use?

What figurative language can I identify? How does each technique contribute to meaning?

What is emphasized through structure? Why?

What is emphasized through repetition? Why is this repeated?

Are there any patterns? Rhyme? Rhythm? When are they broken?

How does sound create mood? Why?

Step 3: Mean Machine Read

Read it aloud again.

What is the overall theme?

How do the sound, words, and shape of this poem work together to create meaning?

title

"The Negro Speaks of Rivers" by Langston Hughes

Source: Hughes, Langston. "The Negro Speaks of Rivers." Poetry.org. *http://www.poets.org/viewmedia.php/prmMID/15722.*

I've known rivers:
I've known rivers ancient as the world and older than the
flow of human blood in human veins.
My soul has grown deep like the rivers.
I bathed in the Euphrates when dawns were young.
I built my hut near the Congo and it lulled me to sleep.
I looked upon the Nile and raised the pyramids above it.
I heard the singing of the Mississippi when Abe Lincoln
went down to New Orleans, and I've seen its muddy
bosom turn all golden in the sunset.
I've known rivers:
Ancient, dusky rivers.
My soul has grown deep like the rivers.

Speaker Black man

think its Sad

Exit Ticket

Self-Assessment

Name: ______________________________

Date: ______________________________

Directions: Please take a moment to reflect on the learning targets of today. Then use your Poet's Toolbox Reference Sheet to complete this Exit Ticket.

1. List the three tools from the Poet's Toolbox with which you are most familiar.

____

____

____

2. List the three tools from the Poet's Toolbox on which you would like more instruction.

____

____

____

3. After seeing the teacher model today's poem, what one specific thing do you think you will struggle with the most as you "pop the hood" on some poems?

____

____

____

Poet's Toolbox Matching Worksheet

Name: ______________________________

Date: ______________________________

Directions: Using your Poet's Toolbox Reference Sheet, match the following poetic lines with their poetic "tool." Remember that some lines may use more than one tool.

Example: What? Like a goat, you ate that hat? simile, consonance

1. You are simply the sun in my sky. ____________
2. Death crept in like a thief and without a word, stole what was most dear to me. ____________
3. Abraham Lincoln, what would you say today? ____________
4. My mother was the rock of our family, my father was like the hot air balloon. ____________
5. When will the winds of fall be still around the tall oak that fell? ____________
6. Courage, we had and strength enough. ____________
7. Wishy-washy ____________
8. He came in, like a whirlwind. ____________
9. He was like a modern-day Moses. ____________
10. I remember the burning ember of late September. ____________
11. Seeing slithering snakes makes my spine shiver. ____________
12. O, Life, why are you so hard? ____________
13. While my elementary school was like picking at cotton candy, junior high was more like trying to eat a caramel apple with braces. ____________
14. When I ran away, I ran fast, and I ran fearfully, and I ran far. ____________
15. Bright, the sun and cool, the water at the beach that day. ____________
16. She tried not to cry but eventually sighed and asked why. ____________

EXPEDITIONARY LEARNING

"If We Must Die" by Claude McKay

Source: McKay, Claude. "If We Must Die." Poetry.org. http://www.poets.org/viewmedia.php/prmMID/15250.

If we must die, let it not be like hogs
Hunted and penned in an inglorious spot,
While round us bark the mad and hungry dogs,
Making their mock at our accursèd lot.
If we must die, O let us nobly die,
So that our precious blood may not be shed
In vain; then even the monsters we defy
Shall be constrained to honor us though dead!
O kinsmen! we must meet the common foe!
Though far outnumbered let us show us brave,
And for their thousand blows deal one death-blow!
What though before us lies the open grave?
Like men we'll face the murderous, cowardly pack,
Pressed to the wall, dying, but fighting back!

EXPEDITIONARY
LEARNING

Poetic Tools in the *Narrative*

Name: ____________________

Date: ____________________

From *Narrative of the Life of Frederick Douglass,* Chapter 6

Background: Frederick Douglass leaves the plantation, happily, and is sent to live with Hugh and Sophia Auld in Baltimore. They want him to be a caretaker for their young son. Living in the city is much different from living on the plantation, and Douglass is astounded at the kind treatment he receives from Mrs. Auld, who has never owned slaves.

From Chapter 6	Second Read Questions	Third Read Questions
1. My new mistress proved to be all she appeared when I first met her at the door,—a woman of the kindest heart and finest feelings. She had never had a slave under her control previously to myself, and prior to her marriage she had been dependent upon her own industry for a living. She was by trade a weaver; and by constant application to her business, she had been in a good degree preserved from the **blighting** and **dehumanizing** effects of slavery. I was utterly astonished at her goodness. I scarcely knew how to behave towards her. She was entirely unlike any other white woman I had ever seen. I could not approach her as I was accustomed to approach other white ladies. My early instruction was all out of place. The **crouching servility**, usually so acceptable a quality in a slave, did not answer when manifested toward her. Her favor was not gained by it; she seemed to be disturbed by it. She did not deem it **impudent** or unmannerly for a slave to look her in the face. The **meanest** slave was put fully at ease in her presence, and none left without feeling better for having seen her. <u>Her face was made of heavenly smiles, and her voice of tranquil music.</u>	**Blighting:** damaging **Dehumanizing:** treating someone very badly **Crouching servility:** being extremely submissive, bowing before someone **Impudent:** disrespectful **Meanest:** lowest class 1. Underline words or phrases that describe Mrs. Auld (the mistress). 2. How did she act toward slaves?	1. What is his mistress (Mrs. Auld) like? 2. What poetic tool(s) does Douglass use to reinforce her personality? 3. How does the tool support his idea?

2. But, alas! this kind heart had but a short time to remain such. The fatal poison of irresponsible power was already in her hands, and soon **commenced** its infernal work. That cheerful eye, under the influence of slavery, soon became red with rage; that voice, made all of sweet accord, changed to one of harsh and horrid discord; and that angelic face gave place to that of a demon.	3. What is the *fatal poison of irresponsible power*? **Commenced:** began 4. Define *discord* vs. *accord.*	4. What happens to Mrs. Auld? 5. What poetic tool(s) does Douglass use to reinforce this idea? 6. How does each support his idea?
3. Very soon after I went to live with Mr. and Mrs. Auld, she very kindly commenced to teach me the A, B, C. After I had learned this, she assisted me in learning to spell words of three or four letters. Just at this point of my progress, Mr. Auld found out what was going on, and at once forbade Mrs. Auld to instruct me further, telling her, among other things, that it was unlawful, as well as unsafe, to teach a slave to read. To use his own words, further, he said, "If you give a nigger an inch, he will take an ell. A nigger should know nothing but to obey his master—to do as he is told to do. Learning would spoil the best nigger in the world. Now," said he, "if you teach that nigger (speaking of myself) how to read, there would be no keeping him. It would forever unfit him to be a slave. He would at once become unmanageable, and of no value to his master. As to himself, it could do him no good, but a great deal of harm. It would make him discontented and unhappy." These words sank deep into my heart, stirred up sentiments within that lay slumbering, and called into existence an entirely new train of	5. What does Mr. Auld tell his wife about teaching a slave to read? 6. Why would teaching a slave to read make him "unfit"?	7. What does Mr. Auld's advice teach Douglass? 8. What poetic tool(s) does Douglass use to reinforce this idea? 9. How does each support his idea?

thought. It was a new and special revelation, explaining dark and mysterious things, with which my youthful understanding had struggled, but struggled in vain. I now understood what had been to me a most perplexing difficulty—to wit, the white man's power to enslave the black man. It was a grand achievement, and I prized it highly. From that moment, I understood the pathway from slavery to freedom.		
4. Though conscious of the difficulty of learning without a teacher, I set out with high hope, and a fixed purpose, at whatever cost of trouble, to learn how to read. The very decided manner with which he spoke, and strove to impress his wife with the evil consequences of giving me instruction, served to convince me that he was deeply sensible of the truths he was uttering. It gave me the best assurance that I might rely with the utmost confidence on the results which, he said, would flow from teaching me to read. What he most dreaded, that I most desired. What he most loved, that I most hated. That which to him was a great evil, to be carefully shunned, was to me a great good, to be diligently sought; and the argument which he so warmly urged, against my learning to read, only served to inspire me with a desire and determination to learn. In learning to read, I owe almost as much to the bitter opposition of my master, as to the kindly aid of my mistress. I acknowledge the benefit of both.	7. What does Douglass resolve to do?	10. Douglass uses **juxtaposition** to compare his decision to Mr. Auld's decision to forbid him to read. How does this help illustrate how committed he is to learning to read?

5. My mistress was, as I have said, a kind and tender-hearted woman; and in the simplicity of her soul she commenced, when I first went to live with her, to treat me as she supposed one human being ought to treat another. In entering upon the duties of a slaveholder, she did not seem to perceive that I sustained to her the relation of a mere **chattel**, and that for her to treat me as a human being was not only wrong, but dangerously so. Slavery proved as **injurious** to her as it did to me. When I went there, she was a pious, warm, and tender-hearted woman. There was no sorrow or suffering for which she had not a tear. She had bread for the hungry, clothes for the naked, and comfort for every mourner that came within her reach. Slavery soon proved its ability to divest her of these heavenly qualities. Under its influence, the tender heart became stone, and the lamblike disposition gave way to one of tiger-like fierceness. The first step in her downward course was in her ceasing to instruct me. She now commenced to practice her husband's precepts. She finally became even more violent in her opposition than her husband himself. She was not satisfied with simply doing as well as he had commanded; she seemed anxious to do better.	**Chattel:** tangible property that can be moved 8. Define *injurious*. 9. How does Mrs. Auld treat Douglass after her husband tells her Douglass mustn't learn to read?	11. Compare Mrs. Auld before and after she owned slaves. 12. What poetic tool(s) does Douglass use to reinforce this idea? 13. How does each support his idea?

Exit Ticket

Poetic Tools in the *Narrative*

Name: ______________________________

Date: ______________________________

Directions: On a scale of 1 to 5, rate how difficult it was for you to complete this assignment today. Explain your choice.

Comprehending the reading:

____

____

____

____

Recognizing the poetic tools:

____

____

____

____

Poetry Analysis Practice 1

Name: ______________________________

Date: ______________________________

Directions: Do a Paint Job Read of this poem. Remember to read it aloud to yourself first. Then annotate the text as you ask yourself the paint job questions. After that, do a second read and underline words or phrases that "pull" you. Write in the margins why these things stand out to you.

"Black Woman" by Georgia Douglas Johnson

Source: Johnson, Georgia Douglas Camp. "Black Woman." Bronze: A Book of Verse. *Editors. Georgia Douglas Camp Johnson and William Edward Burghardt Du Bois. Cambridge: Harvard University Press.*

Don't knock at the door, little child,
I cannot let you in,
You know not what a world this is
Of cruelty and sin.
Wait in the still eternity
Until I come to you,
The world is cruel, cruel, child,
I cannot let you in!
Don't knock at my heart, little one,
I cannot bear the pain
Of turning deaf-ear to your call
Time and time again!
You do not know the monster men
Inhabiting the earth,
Be still, be still, my precious child,
I must not give you birth!

Entry Task

"Black Woman" by Georgia Douglas Johnson

Name: ______________________________

Date: ______________________________

Directions: Reflect on your homework assignment.

1. What parts of the Paint Job Read were difficult for you? Why?

____

____

____

2. Could you identify the speaker? What words or clues helped you?

____

____

____

3. What words or phrases "pulled" you? Why?

____

____

____

4. Can you identify three examples of repetition in this poem?

____

____

____

Source: Johnson, Georgia Douglas Camp. "Black Woman." Bronze: A Book of Verse. *Editors. Georgia Douglas Camp Johnson and William Edward Burghardt Du Bois. Cambridge: Harvard University Press.*

Don't knock at the door, little child,
I cannot let you in,
You know not what a world this is
Of cruelty and sin.
Wait in the still eternity
Until I come to you,
The world is cruel, cruel, child,
I cannot let you in!

Don't knock at my heart, little one,
I cannot bear the pain
Of turning deaf-ear to your call
Time and time again!
You do not know the monster men
Inhabiting the earth,
Be still, be still, my precious child,
I must not give you birth!

"slaveships" by Lucille Clifton

Source: Lucille Clifton, "slaveships" from The Collected Poems of Lucille Clifton. *Copyright © 1996 by Lucile Clifton. Reprinted with permission of The Permissions Company, Inc., on behalf of BOA Editions Ltd., www.boaeditions.org.*

Name: ____

Date: ____

Individual Analysis

Directions: Using the How to Read a Poem Anchor Chart, analyze and annotate this poem.

loaded like spoons
into the belly of Jesus
where we lay for weeks for months
in the sweat and stink of our own
breathing
Jesus
why do you not protect us
chained to the heart of the Angel
where the prayers we never tell
are hot and red as our bloody ankles
Jesus
Angel
can these be men
who vomit us out from ships
called Jesus Angel Grace of God
onto a heathen country
Jesus
Angel
ever again
can this tongue speak
can this bone walk
Grace of God
can this sin live

Partner Read

Directions: Read the poem aloud once again. Using the How to Read a Poem Anchor Chart, share your ideas with your partner and then write down your most brilliant pieces of analysis for each category.

How to Read a Poem	Our Group Discussion
Paint Job Read	
Pop the Hood Read	
Mean Machine Read	

Exit Ticket

Self-Assessment 2

Name: ______________________________

Date: ______________________________

Directions: Reflect on your learning process today and answer the following questions.

1. What do you understand about slavery after reading the poems from today?

____

____

____

2. What part of the How to Read a Poem Anchor Chart did you struggle with today? Why?

____

____

____

3. What part of the How to Read a Poem Anchor Chart did you feel more confident with today? Why?

____

____

____

EXPEDITIONARY
LEARNING

Poetry Analysis Practice 2

Name: ____

Date: ____

Directions: Read the following poem. Annotate the text as you read and follow the How to Read a Poem Anchor Chart. When you get to the Mean Machine Read, record your ideas.

"Harriet Tubman" by Eloise Greenfield

Source: Greenfield, Eloise. "Harriet Tubman." Poetry.org. http://www.poets.org/viewmedia.php/prmMID/16485.

Harriet Tubman didn't take no stuff
Wasn't scared of nothing neither
Didn't come in this world to be no slave
And wasn't going to stay one either

"Farewell!" she sang to her friends one night
She was mighty sad to leave 'em
But she ran away that dark, hot night
Ran looking for her freedom
She ran to the woods and she ran through the woods
With the slave catchers right behind her
And she kept on going till she got to the North
Where those mean men couldn't find her

Nineteen times she went back South
To get three hundred others
She ran for her freedom nineteen times
To save Black sisters and brothers
Harriet Tubman didn't take no stuff
Wasn't scared of nothing neither
Didn't come in this world to be no slave
And didn't stay one either

And didn't stay one either

Mean Machine Questions

1. What is the central idea, or theme, of this poem?

____

____

____

2. Think about the author's use of figurative language, structure, and sound. Which tool(s) most helped you understand the theme? Why?

____

____

____

Entry Task

"Harriet Tubman" by Eloise Greenfield

Name: ______________________________

Date: ______________________________

Directions: Look at your homework and answer the following questions.

1. What **repetition** did you notice in this poem? Could you identify three separate examples?

____

____

____

2. Pick one of these words, sounds, and/or lines and explain why it was emphasized.

____

____

____

3. Did you notice the author included the last line twice? What is the effect of "echoing" this line?

____

____

____

4. Did you notice this poem seems to have two "**speakers**"? What were they? What specific words made them sound different?

____

____

____

5. Was this poem more difficult or less difficult to analyze than the poems you read in class? Why?

____

____

____

6. What other questions do you have?

____

____

____

EXPEDITIONARY LEARNING

End-of-Unit Assessment

Reading Poetry

Analyzing Structure and Language in "We Wear the Mask"

Source: Dunbar, Paul Laurence. "We Wear the Mask." The Collected Poetry of Paul Laurence Dunbar. *Ed. Joanne M. Braxton. Charlottesville: University Press of Virginia, 1993.*

Darion Bell
Jan 8/2018

We Wear the Mask
by Paul Laurence Dunbar

We wear the mask that grins and lies,
It hides our cheeks and shades our eyes,—
This debt we pay to human guile;
With torn and bleeding hearts we smile
And mouth with myriad subtleties,

Stanza 1 gist
I think its tailking about Dugless mom.

Why should the world be over-wise,
In counting all our tears and sighs?
Nay, let them only see us, while
We wear the mask.

Stanza 2 gist
his mom been crying all the time.

We smile, but oh great Christ, our cries
To thee from tortured souls arise.
We sing, but oh the clay is vile
Beneath our feet, and long the mile,
But let the world dream otherwise,
We wear the mask!

Stanza 3 gist
they have nothing to live for.

guile: cleverly deceiving someone
subtleties: not easily noticed
thee: an old-fashioned way of saying "you"; implies respect

EXPEDITIONARY
LEARNING

Paint Job Questions

1. What is the "story" of this poem? Annotate each stanza for the gist in the box provided. (RL.7.5)

they have masks on and they cant see their eyes.

2. Explain how Stanza 2 relates to Stanza 1. (RL.7.5)

it says tears ans sighs with bleeding hearts we smille.

3. Explain how Stanza 3 relates to Stanza 2. (RL.7.5)

we smile, but oh great christ, ourcries why should the world be over-wise in counting all our tears.

4. Describe the speaker of this poem and cite some evidence to support your ideas. (RL.7.1)

We wear the mask when they die

5. What is your first impression of the theme? (RL.7.2)

What does it mean to wear the mask that grins and lies.

Pop the Hood Questions

Form

6. What are two ways that Lines 9 and 15 are different from the rest of the poem? (RL.7.4)

it says we smile, but oh great Christ, our cries to thee from tortured souls arise.

7. Why would the author emphasize these lines? (RL.7.4)

i think they don't care about things.

Figurative Language

8. Underline three words or phrases that "pull" you as a reader. In the margin of the poem, write why you think they are important. (RL.7.1)

we smile but oh great christ our cries to thee from tortured souls arise.

9. Line 10 contains which of the following figurative language? (RL7.4, L.5a)

a. Apostrophe
(b.) Personification
c. Metaphor

Explain your choice.

I think its tailking about somebody is triying to steal masks and the die.

How does this contribute to the theme of the poem?

they wear masks that grins and lies It hides our cheeks and shades.

10. This poem has an **extended metaphor**. (RL.7.4, L.5a)

What is that metaphor?

What are they tailking about wear wear the mask

How does it contribute to the theme of the poem?

why should the world be in over-wise in counting all our tears and sighs.

11. What is the effect of using the pronoun *we* instead of *I* throughout this poem? (L.7.5)

Why they smile, in to thee from to thee from tortured souls arise.

Sound

12. There is a dominant long *i* sound in this poem. Identify five words with this sound. (RL.7.4)

i wear the mask i follow my
on path i do what i have to do things
own my own i do thing my own way.

13. Given the theme, why would the author choose to repeat the long *i* sound? (RL.7.4)

Becaus it says it in his
Poem.

14. What is the rhyme scheme of this poem? (RL.7.4)

we wear the mask that grins and lies
it hides our Cheeks and our eyes.

Mean Machine Questions

15. Think about the author's use of figurative language, structure, and sound. Which tool(s) contributed the most to articulating the theme? Why? (RL.7.2, RL.7.1, RL.7.5, RL.7.4)

it was tallking about his life
what he did.

Narrative Arc Anchor Chart

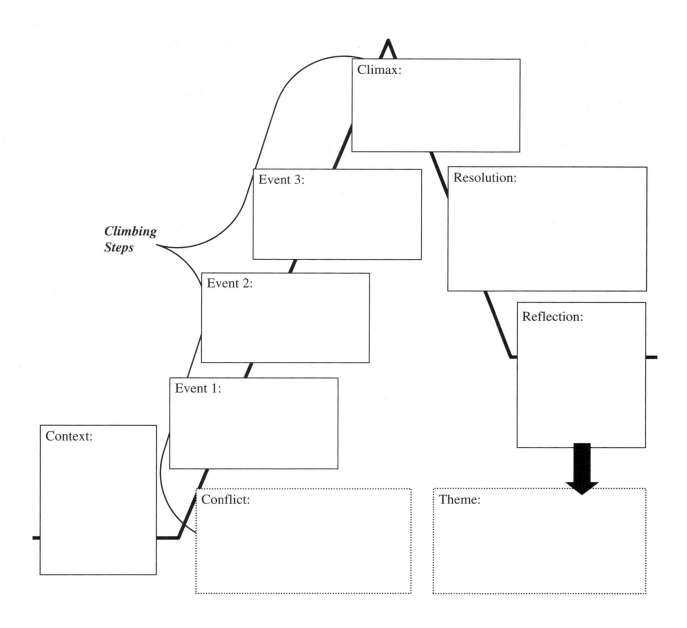

Name: ______________________________

Date: ______________________________

Climax:

Event 3:

Resolution:

Climbing Steps

Event 2:

Reflection:

Event 1:

Context:

Conflict:

Theme:

The Last Day of Slavery Matching Cards

Time: Birth through 17 years old Place: Plantation Characters: Douglass, mother, Covey	Douglass fights Covey and wins.
Covey vs. Douglass	Douglass runs away because he is tired of being beaten.
Douglass's mother dies	Douglass is forced to work harder as he gets older.
Douglass stands up to Covey	Just because you are born into a role does not mean you are destined to be in that role.
Douglass vows to never act or think like a slave again.	

Anatomy of a Sentence Anchor Chart

Name: ______________________________

Date: ______________________________

The dog jumped over the white fence.

Main Clause

- A sentence has at least one independent clause, which includes a subject and a verb.
  - **Verb:** action
  - **Subject:** person/object/place/idea doing the action
- The core of a sentence is its main clause, which is always an independent clause.

Modifiers

- Phrases and dependent clauses modify different words or parts of the sentence, and are usually set apart by a comma.
  - **Modify:** add detail to, clarify

Combining Sentences

- If you have more than one independent clause, you need to connect them with a conjunction or a semicolon; you can also separate them into different sentences.
  - **Conjunction:** a word that connects words or clauses, such as *and, so, but, yet*
- If a sentence does not have both a subject and a verb, it is a sentence fragment.
- We often put commas between adjectives but not between an adjective and a noun.
  - For example: The scruffy, hungry dog ran away.

Example Sentences

1. One sunny morning, the boy picked up his green backpack and, thinking about the friends who were waiting for him at school, walked quickly to the bus stop.
2. Since he was worried about missing the bus, he left a little earlier than usual.
3. While walking to the bus stop, he thought about what position he would play in the soccer match that afternoon.

EXPEDITIONARY LEARNING

Entry Task

Sentence Structure

Name: ______________________________

Date: ______________________________

Directions, Part 1: Complete this task as a class.

1. One sunny morning, the boy picked up his green backpack and, thinking about the friends who were waiting for him at school, walked quickly to the bus stop.
    - Underline the main clause.
    - What does the word *sunny* modify?
2. Since he was worried about missing the bus, he left a little earlier than usual.
    - Underline the main clause.
    - What does the word *little* modify?
3. While walking to the bus stop, he thought about what position he would play in the soccer match that afternoon.
    - Underline the main clause.
    - What does the phrase *while walking to the bus stop* modify?

Directions, Part 2: Complete this task in pairs.

1. Day after day, the girl would dream of getting some playing time during the middle school basketball games.
    - Underline the main clause.
    - What does the phrase *day after day* modify?
2. While the rest of the team went to see a movie, she continued to work on her shooting skills, stopping only once she realized the gym was about to close.
    - Underline the main clause.
    - What does the phrase *while the rest of the team went to see a movie* modify?
3. She practiced her beloved basketball game day and night, and little by little she improved.
    - Underline the main clause.
    - What does the word *beloved* modify?

Text and Questions (Excerpt 3): Learning to Read

Narrative of the Life of Frederick Douglass

Source: Douglass, Frederick. Narrative of the Life of Frederick Douglass. *Boston, Massachusetts: Anti-Slavery Office, 1845. Project Gutenberg. http://www.gutenberg.org/files/23/23-h/23-h.htm.*

Name: ______________________________

Date: ______________________________

Chapter 5, Paragraphs 11–12; Chapter 6, Paragraphs 1–4; Chapter 7, Paragraphs 1–6

Background: Frederick Douglass happily leaves the plantation and is sent to live with Hugh and Sophia Auld in Baltimore. Living in the city is much different from living on the plantation.

Text	Second Read Questions	Third Read Questions
1. I look upon my departure from Colonel Lloyd's plantation as one of the most interesting events of my life. It is possible, and even quite probable, that but for the **mere** circumstance of being removed from that plantation to Baltimore, I should have to-day, instead of being here seated by my own table, in the enjoyment of freedom and the happiness of home, writing this Narrative, been confined in the **galling** chains of slavery.	**Mere:** unimportant **Galling:** making you feel upset and angry because of something that is unfair	

Going to live at Baltimore laid the foundation, and opened the gateway, to all my **subsequent** prosperity. I have ever regarded it as the first plain **manifestation** of that kind **providence** which has ever since attended me, and marked my life with so many favors. I regarded the selection of myself as being somewhat remarkable. There were a number of slave children that might have been sent from the plantation to Baltimore. There were those younger, those older, and those of the same age. I was chosen from among them all, and was the first, last, and only choice.	**Subsequent:** **Manifestation:** clear sign **Providence:** a force that is believed by some people to control what happens in our lives and to protect us 1. How does Douglass feel about his move to Baltimore?	
2. My new mistress proved to be all she appeared when I first met her at the door,—a woman of the kindest heart and finest feelings. She had never had a slave under her control previously to myself, and prior to her marriage she had been dependent upon her own industry for a living. She was by trade a weaver; and by constant application to her business, she had been in a good degree preserved from the **blighting** and **dehumanizing** effects of slavery. I was utterly astonished at her goodness. I scarcely knew how to behave towards her. She was entirely unlike any other white woman I had ever seen. I could not approach her as I was accustomed to approach other white ladies. My early instruction was all out of place.	**Blighting:** damaging **Dehumanizing:** treating people so badly that they lose their good human qualities Douglass feels happy about his move to Baltimore.	
The **crouching servility**, usually so acceptable a quality in a slave, did not answer when manifested toward her. Her favor was not gained by it; she seemed to be disturbed by it. She did not deem it **impudent** or unmannerly for a slave to look her in the face. The **meanest** slave was put fully at ease in her presence, and none left without feeling better for having seen her. Her face was made of heavenly smiles, and her voice of tranquil music.	**Crouching servility:** being extremely submissive, bowing before someone **Impudent:** disrespectful **Meanest:** lowest class	1. What does the word *tranquil* mean? What does Douglass convey about Mrs. Auld when he writes about her "voice of tranquil music"?

3. But, alas! this kind heart had but a short time to remain such. The fatal poison of irresponsible power was already in her hands, and soon **commenced** its infernal work. That cheerful eye, under the influence of slavery, soon became red with rage; that voice, made all of sweet accord, changed to one of harsh and horrid discord; and that angelic face gave place to that of a demon.	**Commenced:** began	2. Douglass juxtaposes Mrs. Auld before and after becoming a slaveholder. Write down some examples of the language Douglass uses to make this comparison. Who or what does Douglass blame for the transformation of Mrs. Auld? How do you know?
4. Very soon after I went to live with Mr. and Mrs. Auld, she very kindly commenced to teach me the A, B, C. After I had learned this, she assisted me in learning to spell words of three or four letters. Just at this point of my progress, Mr. Auld found out what was going on, and at once **forbade** Mrs. Auld to instruct me further, telling her, among other things, that it was unlawful, as well as unsafe, to teach a slave to read. To use his own words, further, he said, "If you give a nigger an inch, he will take an ell. A nigger should know nothing but to obey his master—to do as he is told to do. Learning would spoil the best nigger in the world." "Now," said he, "if you teach that nigger (speaking of myself) how to read, there would be no keeping him. It would forever unfit him to be a slave.	**Forbade:** to tell someone to stop doing something. Douglass wants the reader to know that slaveholders are scared to let slaves know how to read.	3. Mr. Auld claimed that if you teach a slave how to read, "there would be no keeping him. It would forever unfit him to be a slave." What does Mr. Auld think that reading will do to a slave? What does Douglass convey about the attitude of slaveholders toward slaves by including this quote? Mr auld thinks reading will make the slaves think

He would at once become unmanageable, and of no value to his master. As to himself, it could do him no good, but a great deal of harm. It would make him discontented and unhappy." These words sank deep into my heart, stirred up **sentiments** within that lay slumbering, and called into existence an entirely new train of **revelation**, explaining dark and mysterious things, with which my youthful understanding had struggled, but struggled in vain. I now understood what had been to me a most perplexing difficulty—to wit, the white man's power to enslave the black man. It was a grand achievement, and I prized it highly. From that moment, I understood the pathway from slavery to freedom.	**Sentiments:** opinions or feelings **Revelation:** an idea that is new or surprising he set out with high hope and a fixed purpose to learn how to aware.	
5. Though conscious of the difficulty of learning without a teacher, I set out with high hope, and a fixed purpose, at whatever cost of trouble, to learn how to read. The very decided manner with which he spoke, and strove to impress his wife with the evil consequences of giving me instruction, served to convince me that he was deeply **sensible** of the truths he was uttering. It gave me the best assurance that I might rely with the utmost confidence on the results which, he said, would flow from teaching me to read. What he most dreaded, that I most desired. What he most loved, that I most hated. That which to him was a great evil, to be carefully shunned, was to me a great good, to be diligently sought; and the argument which he so warmly urged, against my learning to read, only served to inspire me with a desire and determination to learn. In learning to read, I owe almost as much to the bitter opposition of my master, as to the kindly aid of my mistress. I acknowledge the benefit of both.	2. What is Douglass determined to do? **Sensible:** aware	

6. My mistress was, as I have said, a kind and tender-hearted woman; and in the simplicity of her soul she commenced, when I first went to live with her, to treat me as she supposed one human being ought to treat another. In entering upon the duties of a slaveholder, she did not seem to perceive that I sustained to her the relation of a mere **chattel**, and that for her to treat me as a human being was not only wrong, but dangerously so. Slavery proved as **injurious** to her as it did to me. When I went there she was a pious, warm, and tender-hearted woman. There was no sorrow or suffering for which she had not a tear. She had bread for the hungry, clothes for the naked, and comfort for every mourner that came within her reach. Slavery soon proved its ability to **divest** her of these heavenly qualities.	**Chattel:** tangible property that can be moved **Injurious:** doing harm 3. What was Mrs. Auld like before she owned slaves? What was she like after owning a slave? **Divest:** remove or take away	
Under its influence, the tender heart became stone, and the lamblike disposition gave way to one of tiger-like fierceness. The first step in her downward course was in her ceasing to instruct me. She now commenced to practice her husband's **precepts**. She finally became even more violent in her opposition than her husband himself. She was not satisfied with simply doing as well as he had commanded; she seemed anxious to do better.	**Precepts:**	
7. From this time I was most narrowly watched. If I was in a separate room any considerable length of time, I was sure to be suspected of having a book, and was at once called to give an account of myself. All this, however, was too late. The first step had been taken. **Mistress**, in teaching me the alphabet, had given me the inch, and no precaution could prevent me from taking the ell.	4. Who was watching Douglass? Why were they watching him? **Mistress:** used with a woman's family name as a polite way of speaking to her 5. In this case what was Douglass given by his "mistress" and what did he want more of?	4. How do the Aulds want Douglass to feel about continuing to learn to read and how do you know?

8. The plan which I adopted, and the one by which I was most successful, was that of making friends of all the little white boys whom I met in the street. As many of these as I could, I **converted** into teachers. With their kindly aid, **obtained** at different times and in different places, I finally succeeded in learning to read. When I was sent of errands, I always took my book with me, and by going one part of my errand quickly, I found time to get a lesson before my return. I used also to carry bread with me, enough of which was always in the house, and to which I was always welcome; for I was much better off in this regard than many of the poor white children in our neighborhood.	**Converted:** **Obtained:**	
This bread I used to bestow upon the hungry little **urchins**, who, in return, would give me that more **valuable** bread of knowledge. I am strongly tempted to give the names of two or three of those little boys, as a testimonial of the gratitude and affection I bear them; but **prudence** forbids;—not that it would injure me, but it might embarrass them; for it is almost an unpardonable offence to teach slaves to read in this Christian country. It is enough to say of the dear little fellows, that they lived on Philpot Street, very near Durgin and Bailey's **ship-yard**. I used to talk this matter of slavery over with them. I would sometimes say to them, I wished I could be as free as they would be when they got to be men. "You will be free as soon as you are twenty-one, but I am a slave for life! Have not I as good a right to be free as you have?" These words used to trouble them; they would express for me the liveliest sympathy, and console me with the hope that something would occur by which I might be free.	**Urchin:** a poor, dirty child 6. Douglass uses the word *valuable,* which has the suffix *-able,* which means "capable of." What does he mean when he describes the bread of knowledge as valuable? **Prudence:** a careful attitude that makes you avoid unnecessary risks **Ship-yard:** a place where ships are built or repaired 7. List some ways that Douglass continued to learn to read.	

<table>
<tr>
<td>9. The more I read, the more I was led to abhor and detest my enslavers. I could regard them in no other light than a band of successful robbers, who had left their homes, and gone to Africa, and stolen us from our homes, and in a strange land reduced us to slavery. I loathed them as being the meanest as well as the most wicked of men.</td>
<td>8. Choose a group of context clues that best helps you determine the meaning of the words abhor and detest:
enslavers, robbers, reduced us to slavery
read, light, gone to Africa, strange land
homes, gone to Africa, strange land
read, strange land, reduced
9. Douglass uses the word reduced, which has the prefix re-, which means "back." What does Douglass mean when he writes he was "reduced to slavery"?</td>
<td>5. After learning to read himself, would Douglass agree with Mr. Auld's opinion about slaves learning to read? (Refer back to the quote from Paragraph 4.)</td>
</tr>
<tr>
<td>As I read and contemplated the subject, behold! that very discontentment which Master Hugh had predicted would follow my learning to read had already come, to torment and sting my soul to unutterable anguish. As I writhed under it, I would at times feel that learning to read had been a curse rather than a blessing. It had given me a view of my wretched condition, without the remedy.</td>
<td>10. Douglass uses the word discontentment to describe how he felt after learning to read. The prefix dis- means "to take away." What does the word discontentment mean?</td>
<td></td>
</tr>
</table>

	Wretched: very unhappy 11. Paraphrase this sentence in your own words: "It had given me a view of my wretched condition, without the remedy."	
It opened my eyes to the **horrible pit**, but to no ladder upon which to get out. In moments of agony, I envied my fellow-slaves for their stupidity. I have often wished myself a beast. I preferred the condition of the meanest reptile to my own. Any thing, no matter what, to get rid of thinking! It was this everlasting thinking of my condition that tormented me. There was no getting rid of it. It was pressed upon me by every object within sight or hearing, animate or inanimate. The silver trump of freedom had roused my soul to eternal wakefulness. Freedom now appeared, to disappear no more forever. It was heard in every sound, and seen in every thing. It was ever present to torment me with a sense of my wretched condition. I saw nothing without seeing it, I heard nothing without hearing it, and felt nothing without feeling it. It looked from every star, it smiled in every calm, breathed in every wind, and moved in every storm.	12. How did learning how to read affect Douglass's view on being enslaved?	6. What does Douglass compare to a "**horrible pit**"? What type of figurative language is this and how does it affect the tone of the paragraph? a. personification b. vivid word choice c. metaphor d. allusion

10. I often found myself regretting my own existence, and wishing myself dead; and but for the hope of being free, I have no doubt but that I should have killed myself, or done something for which I should have been killed. While in this state of mind, I was eager to hear any one speak of slavery. I was a ready listener. Every little while, I could hear something about the abolitionists. It was some time before I found what the word meant. It was always used in such connections as to make it an interesting word to me. If a slave ran away and succeeded in getting clear, or if a slave killed his master, set fire to a barn, or did anything very wrong in the mind of a slaveholder, it was spoken of as the fruit of **abolition**. Hearing the word in this connection very often, I set about learning what it meant.	13. Why is Douglass so interested in figuring out what *abolition* means? **Abolition:**	7. In the *Freedom: History of US* text from Unit 1, you read the following about Douglass, "He saw the terrible things that happen when one person has complete control over another." In what ways have slaves been controlled by slaveholders in this excerpt and in others? How do these examples of control serve Douglass's purpose?
The dictionary **afforded** me little or no help. I found it was "the act of abolishing"; but then I did not know what was to be abolished. Here I was perplexed. I did not dare to ask any one about its meaning, for I was satisfied that it was something they wanted me to know very little about. After a patient waiting, I got one of our city papers, containing an account of the number of petitions from the north, praying for the abolition of slavery in the District of Columbia, and of the slave trade between the States. From this time I understood the words **abolition** and **abolitionist,** and always drew near when that word was spoken, expecting to hear something of importance to myself and fellow-slaves. The light broke in upon me by degrees.	**Afforded:** provided	8. After Douglass figures out what *abolition* means, he says, "The light broke in upon me by degrees." What does this mean and what type of figurative language is this? How does it show the importance of this moment in Douglass's life? a. personification b. vivid word choice c. metaphor/simile d. allusion

Whole Excerpt

PURPOSE: How does this excerpt support the two positions Douglass held about slavery that are listed here?

1. Slavery is terrible for slaves.
   its bad for there improvirement.

2. Slavery corrupts slaveholders.
   they should be free and not worlc for them.

EXPEDITIONARY LEARNING

Powerful Language Word Wall

Powerful Language in *Narrative of the Life of Frederick Douglass*

Word choice		Figurative language	
Note card with example	**Note card with example**	**Note card with example**	**Note card with example**
Note card with example	**Note card with example**	**Note card with example**	**Note card with example**
Note card with example	**Note card with example**	**Note card with example**	**Note card with example**

EXPEDITIONARY
LEARNING

Powerful Language T-Chart

Name: ______________________________

Date: ______________________________

Directions: Write each word in the column that it belongs in. Complete this task with a partner.

Obvious dislike

Glaring odiousness

Blood-stained gate

Terrible spectacle

Gratification of their wicked desires

Happy because of their bad wishes

Entrance to somewhere bad

Bad sight

POWERFUL (strong)	**BLAND (weak)**

Why does Frederick Douglass use such powerful language in the *Narrative*?

Vivid Word Choice Card Directions

Card Prompt

Word Choice Card
Name:________________
Write the sentence or part of the sentence; underline the powerful word(s) you are focusing on.
Bland words:
Effect on meaning/tone:

Card Example

Word Choice Card
Name:________________
"From an <u>angel</u>, she became a <u>demon</u>"
Bland words: *good person, bad person*
Effect on meaning/tone: *This shows how Mrs. Auld went from one extreme to another once she became a slaveholder.*

Skim Excerpt 3.
Underline words that "pull" you.
Think about the questions:
*What words stick out to me?
*How do they contribute to the tone?
Fill out a word choice card.

Vivid Word Choice Cards

Word Choice Card
Name:____________________
Write the sentence or part of the sentence; underline the powerful word(s) you are focusing on.
Bland words:
Effect on meaning/tone:

Word Choice Card
Name:____________________
Write the sentence or part of the sentence; underline the powerful word(s) you are focusing on.
Bland words:
Effect on meaning/tone:

EXPEDITIONARY LEARNING

Sentence Structure Homework

Name: ______________________________

Date: ______________________________

Directions: Complete this task for homework. Use the Anatomy of a Sentence Anchor Chart or the Entry Task: Sentence Structure (from Lesson 2) to assist you when completing this task. Remember that some sentences may have several main clauses!

Example: Jessica and her friends decided to get some pepperoni and mushroom pizza, since that was their favorite food.	Underline the main clause. What does the word "favorite" modify? *Food*

Although the recreation center was open seven days a week, the public library was open only during the weekdays, so I could not do research on my science project over the weekend.	Underline the main clause. What does the word *public* modify?
I have lived in New York City for almost 20 years, but my neighbor has lived here for 30 years.	Underline the main clause
Once the storm began to approach, the sky was filled with birds; they knew bad weather was approaching, and wanted to seek shelter.	Underline the main clause. What does the word *bad* modify?
These words sank deep into my heart, stirred up sentiments within that lay slumbering, and called into existence an entirely new train of thought.	Underline the main clause. What do the words *lay slumbering* modify?
From that moment, I understood the pathway from slavery to freedom.	Underline the main clause.
When I went there, she was a pious, warm, and tender-hearted woman.	Underline the main clause.
I looked like a man who had escaped a den of wild beasts.	Underline the main clause. What does the word *wild* modify?

Write two sentences of your own and underline the main clause.

EXPEDITIONARY
LEARNING

Analysis Note-Catcher (Excerpt 3): Learning to Read

Narrative of the Life of Frederick Douglass

Name: ____

Date: ____

Chapter 5, Paragraphs 11–12; Chapter 6, Paragraphs 1–4; Chapter 7, Paragraphs 1–6

What does Douglass say? **What is this excerpt about?**	**(See narrative arc on the next page)**	
Position: Why does he say it? Briefly explain the connection between this excerpt and each of the two positions listed below.	**Evidence:** What words, phrases, and sentences show his position? (Choose one or two quotes for each position; give the source and briefly state what each refers to.)	**Analysis:** What is the position that Douglass is trying to disprove? How does this quote prove that this position is incorrect?
Slavery corrupts slave owners. **Slavery was terrible for slaves.**		

Narrative Arc

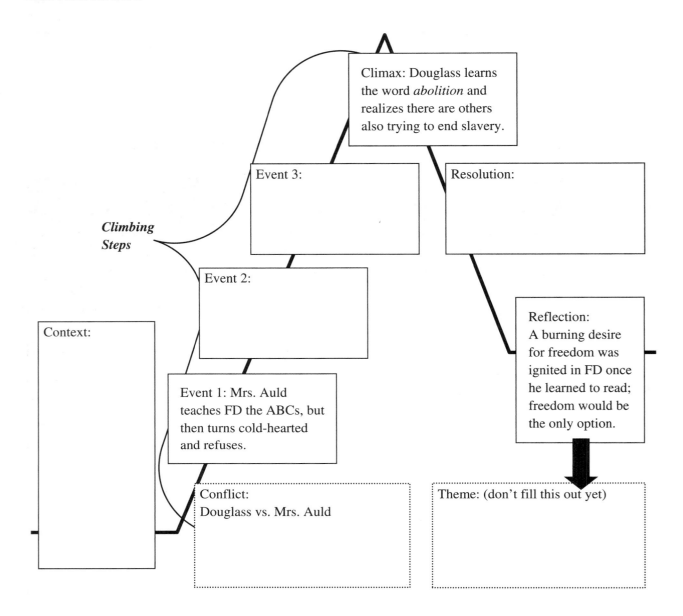

Climax: Douglass learns the word *abolition* and realizes there are others also trying to end slavery.

Climbing Steps

Event 3:

Resolution:

Event 2:

Context:

Reflection:
A burning desire for freedom was ignited in FD once he learned to read; freedom would be the only option.

Event 1: Mrs. Auld teaches FD the ABCs, but then turns cold-hearted and refuses.

Conflict:
Douglass vs. Mrs. Auld

Theme: (don't fill this out yet)

EXPEDITIONARY
LEARNING

Excerpt Analysis Roles

Name: ____________________

Date: ____________________

Independently:

Role 1: Explain the narrative arc.	**Context** of the story (setting—time in Douglass's life, place, and characters)
	Conflict (who the conflict is between)
	Climbing steps (four key events)
	Climax (major turning point)
	Conclusion (resolution—the way Douglass overcomes the obstacles; reflection—how Douglass changes because of the obstacles he encounters)
Role 2: Explain slavery corrupts slave owners.	**Position:** Explain how the excerpt conveys this position.
	Evidence: How does Douglass say it? Write down one or two important quotes and phrases from the text. Explain key people and events and include the paragraph number.
	Analysis: What is the position that Douglass is trying to disprove? How does this quote prove that this position is incorrect?
Role 3: Explain slavery is terrible for slaves.	**Position:** Explain how the excerpt conveys this position.
	Evidence: How does Douglass say it? Write down one or two important quotes and phrases from the text. Explain key people and events and include the paragraph number.
	Analysis: What is the position that Douglass is trying to disprove? How does this quote prove that this position is incorrect?

Together: Share, revise, and fill in the chart.

EXPEDITIONARY LEARNING

Group Work Skits

Name: ______________________________

Date: ______________________________

Scene 1

STUDENT 1: I am working on the narrative arc. Can you both start your sections, so we have time to share afterward?

STUDENT 2: What are we supposed to be doing? I was not really listening. (turns to Student 3) Can you help me?

STUDENT 3: I really want to go shopping at the mall and get some new clothes. What time is this class over?

STUDENT 1: Let me see your paper (takes paper from Student 2). I am going to just fill out the slavery corrupts slaveholders section since you don't know what to do and are taking too long!

STUDENT 2: But I just need help getting started.

STUDENT 3: Forget about this work, I'm hungry, do you have any cookies or chips or anything to eat?

STUDENT 1: But we only have 5 minutes left and we hardly have time to share! Ugh!

Scene 2

STUDENT 1: I am going to be working on the narrative arc; can you both get started on your sections, so we have time to share afterward?

STUDENT 2: What are we supposed to be doing? I was not really listening. (turns to student 3) Can you help me?

STUDENT 3: Sure, so your role is to explain why Douglass included the position slavery corrupts slave owners, find two examples from the text that show this position, and finally explain how the evidence helps Douglass disprove an opposing position. You need to write some notes for each one to hold your thinking. You can also use your notes from the purpose section of our second read to get started on the why section if you need more help.

STUDENT 2: Oh, thanks. That is really helpful. I get it now.

(STUDENTS 2 and 3 work silently)

STUDENT 2: I am done with my section. Are you done with the narrative arc and slavery is terrible for slaves sections?

STUDENT 3: I am! (turns to Student 1) Can you go first and explain about the narrative while we take notes?

STUDENT 1: Sure, I am ready. I will only take a few minutes so you both have time to share also.

STUDENT 2: I think you forgot to include the characters in the setting.

STUDENT 3: Oh yeah, you are right. Let me add Douglass, Mr. Auld, Mrs. Auld, and the little street boys.

EXPEDITIONARY
LEARNING

Excerpt Analysis Group Assignments

Today, the role assignments are

Role	Students with Number
Narrative arc	
Explain that slavery corrupts slave owners.	
Explain that slavery is terrible for slaves.	

GROUP A	Name	GROUP E	Name
Student 1:		Student 1:	
Student 2:		Student 2:	
Student 3:		Student 3:	

GROUP B	Name	GROUP F	Name
Student 1:		Student 1:	
Student 2:		Student 2:	
Student 3:		Student 3:	

GROUP C	Name	GROUP G	Name
Student 1:		Student 1:	
Student 2:		Student 2:	
Student 3:		Student 3:	

GROUP D	Name	GROUP H	Name
Student 1:		Student 1:	
Student 2:		Student 2:	
Student 3:		Student 3:	

EXPEDITIONARY
LEARNING

Constructed Response (Excerpt 3) Tagia

Name: Darion Bell

Date: Feb 18, 2019

Directions: Reread Excerpt 3 from *Narrative of the Life of Frederick Douglass*. Answer the question, "How did learning to read affect Douglass's feelings about being a slave and why? What specific examples from the text support your thinking?"

Reminders:

- Recycle the prompt.
- Give detailed examples from the text.
- Answer all parts of the question.
- Write in complete sentences.

This important because douglass don't like being a slave and he learn that if You teach Slaves how to read they will be free and don't have to be in that situation they are in and he wanted to Know about the slaves hearing the word in this connection very often I set about learning about what it meant, "the act of abolishing"

EXPEDITIONARY
LEARNING

Independent Reading Status Check

Name: Darion Bell

Date: Feb 14, 2019

Did you meet your independent reading goal for today's check-in?	
If yes, what helped you do that?	Sometimes i do it and sometimes i don't
If no, what got in your way? How can I help you?	[illegible]

Storyteller's Toolbox Anchor Chart

Name: Darion Bell

Date: Feb 18/2019

Voice	Body
Tone and volume How does the storyteller's tone reinforce emotion? Is the storyteller talking loudly? When is the storyteller talking softly?	**Facial expression** Is the storyteller's face mirroring the emotion behind the story? Is the storyteller's face helping me picture the character?
Speed Why is the storyteller speeding up or slowing down her voice?	**Hand and body motions** How do the hand motions mimic or reinforce the words?
Repetition What is the storyteller repeating? Why is this an important phrase to remember?	Reinforce or mirror emotion of the characters.

A storyteller uses these tools in order to

Reinforce the action of the story

Reinforce or mirror emotion of the characters

Help the listener picture the action

Text and Questions (Excerpt 4)

"The Fight with Covey"

Narrative of the Life of Frederick Douglass

Source: Douglass, Frederick. Narrative of the Life of Frederick Douglass. *Boston, Massachusetts: Anti-Slavery Office, 1845. Project Gutenberg.*

Name: Darion Bell

Date: Feb 18/2019

Chapter 10, Paragraphs 1–3, 5, 6, 10–13

Background: When he was 16, Douglass was sent to a new master, Thomas Auld, who owned a plantation in St. Michael's, Maryland. Auld found Douglass defiant, and rented him out for one year to a nearby farmer, Edward Covey, who had a reputation for "breaking" slaves.

Text	Second Read Questions	Third Read Questions
1. I had left Master Thomas's house, and went to live with Mr. Covey, on the 1st of January, 1833. I was now, for the first time in my life, a **field hand**.	**Field hand:** someone who works in the fields on a farm	
2. I lived with Mr. Covey one year. During the first six months, of that year, **scarce** a week passed without his whipping me. I was seldom free from a sore back. My awkwardness was almost always his excuse for whipping me. We were worked fully up to the point of **endurance**. Long before day we were up, our horses fed, and by the first approach of day we were off to the field with our hoes and ploughing teams. Mr. Covey gave us enough to eat, but scarce time to eat it. We were often less than five minutes taking our meals. We were often in the field from the first approach of day till its last lingering ray had left us; and at **saving-fodder time**, midnight often caught us in the field binding blades.	**Scarce:** barely **Endurance:** the capacity to do something difficult for a long time **Saving-fodder time:** the weeks in the year when they were cutting the hay and storing it for winter 1. Why does Douglass say that the slaves were worked up to the point of *endurance*? They are week Becaus they got beatting and they did not care if they got the work	1. What type of figurative language does the phrase "midnight often caught us" use? • metaphor • simile • allusion • personification

and that the only way for the slaves to be free is that they have to learn how to read

3. Covey would be out with us. The way he used to stand it, was this. He would spend the most of his afternoons in bed. He would then come out fresh in the evening, ready to **urge us on** with his words, example, and frequently **with the whip**. Mr. Covey was one of the few slaveholders who could and did work with his hands. He was a hard-working man. He knew by himself just what a man or a boy could do. There was no deceiving him. His work went on in his absence almost as well as in his presence; and he had the **faculty** of making us feel that he was ever present with us. This he did by surprising us. He seldom approached the spot where we were at work openly, if he could do it secretly. He always aimed at taking us by surprise.	2. What does it mean to "urge us on . . . with the whip"?" **Faculty:** of making us fell that he was ever present with us.	2. Why does Douglass use the word *cunning* to describe Covey, rather than *intelligence* or *effectiveness*? How does that connect to his purpose in telling this story?
Such was his **cunning**, that we used to call him, among ourselves, "the snake." When we were at work in the cornfield, he would sometimes crawl on his hands and knees to avoid **detection**, and all at once he would rise nearly in our midst, and scream out, "Ha, ha! Come, come! Dash on, dash on!" This being his mode of attack, it was never safe to stop a single minute. His comings were like a thief in the night. He appeared to us as being ever at hand. He was under every tree, behind every stump, in every bush, and at every window, on the plantation.	**Cunning:** **Detection:** 3. How did Covey make sure that the slaves were working hard all the time? this he did by suprising them.	

EXPEDITIONARY LEARNING

4. If at any one time of my life more than another, I was made to drink the bitterest **dregs** of slavery, that time was during the first six months of my stay with Mr. Covey. We were worked in all weathers. It was never too hot or too cold; it could never rain, blow, hail, or snow too hard for us to work in the field. Work, work, work, was scarcely more the order of the day than of the night. The longest days were too short for him, and the shortest nights too long for him. I was somewhat unmanageable when I first went there, but a few months of this discipline tamed me. Mr. Covey succeeded in **breaking** me. I was broken in body, soul, and spirit.	**Dregs:** the last, usually not very good tasting, sips of a drink **Breaking:**	"The longest days were too short for him, and the shortest nights too long for him." 3. What is the name for this type of figurative language? What does this sentence mean? How does it help Douglass make his point about Covey?
My natural elasticity was crushed, my intellect **languished**, the **disposition** to read departed, the cheerful spark that lingered about my eye died; the dark night of slavery closed in upon me; and behold a man transformed into a **brute**!	**Languished:** did poorly 4. The word *disposition* means tendency or frame of mind. What prefix does it use? What root? **Brute:** a beast 5. How did working for Covey affect Douglass? he was braking him	4. Douglass says that the "dark night of slavery closed in on me." What device from the poet's toolbox is he using? Why is darkness a powerful image here? a. simile b. metaphor c. personification d. apostrophe

5. Sunday was my only **leisure** time. I spent this in a sort of beast-like **stupor**, between sleep and wake, under some large tree. At times I would rise up, a flash of energetic freedom would dart through my soul, accompanied with a faint beam of hope, that flickered for a moment, and then vanished. I sank down again, mourning over my **wretched** condition. I was sometimes prompted to **take my life**, and that of Covey, but was prevented by a combination of hope and fear. My sufferings on this plantation seem now like a dream rather than a stern reality.	**Leisure:** **Stupor:** **Wretched:** **Take my life:** kill myself 6. What did Douglass do on Sundays? taken a break to take a day off	
6. I have already **intimated** that my condition was much worse during the first six months of my stay at Mr. Covey's, than in the last six. The circumstances leading to the change in Mr. Covey's course toward me form an **epoch** in my humble history. You have seen how a man was made a slave; you shall see how a slave was made a man.	**Intimated:** suggested **Epoch:** important period of time	"You have seen how a man was made a slave; you shall see how a slave was made a man." 5. How does this sentence preview the rest of the story? What does Douglass want his audience to pay attention to?

7. On one of the hottest days of the month of August 1833, Bill Smith, William Hughes, a slave named Eli, and myself, were engaged in **fanning wheat**. Hughes was clearing the fanned wheat from before the fan. Eli was turning, Smith was feeding, and I was carrying wheat to the fan. The work was simple, requiring strength rather than intellect; yet, to one entirely unused to such work, it came very hard. About three o'clock of that day, I broke down; my strength failed me; I was seized with a violent aching of the head, **attended with** extreme dizziness; I trembled in every limb. Finding what was coming, I nerved myself up, feeling it would never do to stop work. I stood as long as I could stagger to the **hopper** with grain. When I could stand no longer, I fell, and felt as if held down by an **immense** weight. The fan of course stopped; everyone had his own work to do; and no one could do the work of the other and have his own go on at the same time.	**Fanning wheat:** a process of separating the grain part of the wheat from the stalk it grew on, by using a fanning device **Attended with:** accompanied by **Hopper:** the place in the machine where Douglass was loading the wheat **Immense:** 7. Why did Douglass stop working? he had a headac	6. In this paragraph, Douglass describes how terrible he was feeling. List three words or phrases that help create the mood in this paragraph.
8. Mr. Covey was at the house, about one hundred yards from the treading-yard where we were fanning. On hearing the fan stop, he left immediately, and came to the spot where we were. He **hastily** inquired what the matter was. Bill answered that I was sick, and there was no one to bring wheat to the fan. I had by this time crawled away under the side of the post and rail-fence by which the yard was enclosed, hoping to find relief by getting out of the sun. He then asked where I was. He was told by one of the **hands**. He came to the spot, and, after looking at me awhile, asked me what was the matter. I told him as well as I could, for I scarce had strength to speak. He then gave me a savage kick	**Hastily:** quickly **Hands:** workers	7. Why does Douglass describe the kick Covey gave him as "savage" and not "hard"? How does that contribute to the description of the events?

in the side, and told me to get up. I tried to do so, but fell back in the attempt. He gave me another kick, and again told me to rise. I again tried, and succeeded in **gaining my feet**; but, stooping to get the tub with which I was feeding the fan, I again staggered and fell. While down in this situation, Mr. Covey took up the hickory **slat** with which Hughes had been striking off the half-bushel measure, and with it gave me a heavy blow upon the head, making a large wound, and the blood ran freely; and with this again told me to get up. I made no effort to **comply**, having now made up my mind to let him do his worst. In a short time after receiving this blow, my head grew better. Mr. Covey had now left me to my fate.	**Gaining my feet:** standing up **Slat:** piece of wood **Comply:** obey 8. What did Covey do to Douglass when he found him in the shade? beat him with wood	

Douglass at this point decided to go to his master (Thomas Auld, who had rented him to Covey for one year) and ask for help. He walked to his master's, but his master sent him back to Covey the next morning.

Text	Second Read Questions	Third Read Questions
9. I reached Covey's about nine o'clock; and just as I was getting over the fence that divided Mrs. Kemp's fields from ours, out ran Covey with his cowskin, to give me another whipping. Before he could reach me, I succeeded in getting to the cornfield; and as the corn was very high, it **afforded** me the means of hiding. He seemed very angry, and searched for me a long time. My behavior was altogether **unaccountable**. He finally gave up the chase, thinking, I suppose, that I must come home for something to eat; he would give himself no further trouble in looking for me. I spent that day mostly in the woods, having the alternative before me,—to go home and be whipped to death, or stay in the woods and be starved to death.	**Afforded:** **Unaccountable:** unable to be explained 9. What problem would Douglass face if he did not return to Covey? he said no	

10. That night, I **fell in with** Sandy Jenkins, a slave with whom I was somewhat acquainted. Sandy had a free wife who lived about four miles from Mr. Covey's; and it being Saturday, he was on his way to see her. I told him my circumstances, and he very kindly invited me to go home with him. I went home with him, and talked this whole matter over, and got his advice as to what **course** it was best for me **to pursue**. I found Sandy an old adviser. He told me, with great **solemnity**, I must go back to Covey; but that before I went, I must go with him into another part of the woods, where there was a certain *root*, which, if I would take some of it with me, carrying it *always on my right side*, would **render** it impossible for Mr. Covey, or any other white man, to whip me.	**Fell in with:** ran into and spent time with **Course to pursue:** plan to follow **Solemnity:** seriousness **Render:**	
He said he had carried it for years; and since he had done so, he had never received a blow, and never expected to while he carried it. I at first **rejected** the idea, that the simple carrying of a root in my pocket would have any such effect as he had said, and was not **disposed** to take it; but Sandy impressed the necessity with much earnestness, telling me it could do no harm, if it did no good. To please him, I at length took the root, and, according to his direction, carried it upon my right side.	**Rejected:** 10. **Disposition** (Paragraph 4) is a noun, meaning tendency or frame of mind. *Disposed* is the verb. What does it mean? 11. What does Sandy tell Douglass he should do?	Sandy Jenkins, a slave with whom I was somewhat acquainted.
11. This was Sunday morning. I immediately started for home; and upon entering the yard gate, out came Mr. Covey on his way to meeting. He spoke to me very kindly, **bade** me drive the pigs from a lot nearby, and passed on towards the church. Now, this **singular conduct** of Mr. Covey really made me begin to think that there was something in the ROOT which Sandy had given me; and had it been on any other day than Sunday, I could have attributed the conduct to no other cause than the influence of that root; and as it was, I was half inclined to think the *root* to be something more than I at first had taken it to be. All went well till Monday morning. On this morning, the **virtue** of the ROOT was fully tested.	**Bade:** told **Singular conduct:** unusual behavior **Virtue:** power 12. How does Covey behave toward Douglass when he first arrives back at the farm? Covey really made me begin to think that there was something in the root which Sandy had given me.	8. Why does Douglass end the paragraph with the sentence: "On this morning, the virtue of the ROOT was fully tested?" he got beat Root which Sandy had given me and had it been on any other day than Sunday I could have attributed the conduct.

12. Long before daylight, I was called to go and rub, **curry**, and feed, the horses. I obeyed, and was glad to obey. But whilst thus **engaged**, whilst in the act of throwing down some blades from the loft, Mr. Covey entered the stable with a long rope; and just as I was half out of the loft, he caught hold of my legs, and was about tying me. As soon as I found what he was up to, I gave a sudden **spring**, and as I did so, he holding to my legs, I was brought sprawling on the stable floor.	**Curry:** comb and brush **Engaged:** busy **Spring:** jump	9. What details does Douglass provide that portray Covey as a bully and not a fair fighter?
Mr. Covey seemed now to think he had me, and could do what he pleased; but at this moment—from whence came the spirit I don't know—I resolved to fight; and, suiting my action to the resolution, I seized Covey hard by the throat; and as I did so, I rose. He held on to me, and I to him. My resistance was so entirely unexpected that Covey seemed taken all aback. He trembled like a leaf. This gave me **assurance**, and I held him uneasy, causing the blood to run where I touched him with the ends of my fingers. Mr. Covey soon called out to Hughes for help. Hughes came, and, while Covey held me, attempted to tie my right hand. While he was in the act of doing so, I watched my chance, and gave him a heavy kick close under the ribs. This kick fairly sickened Hughes, so that he left me in the hands of Mr. Covey.	13. How does the fight between Douglass and Covey start? 14. Paraphrase the sentence that shows Douglass's response: "Mr. Covey seemed now to think he had me, and could do what he pleased; but at this moment—from whence came the spirit I don't know—I resolved to fight; and, suiting my action to the resolution, I seized Covey hard by the throat; and as I did so, I rose." **Assurance:** confidence	while he was in the act of doing so, I watched my chance, and gave him a heavy kick close under the ribs. this kick fairly sickenc hughes, So that he left me in the hands of mr. covey
This kick had the effect of not only weakening Hughes, but Covey also. When he saw Hughes bending over with pain, his courage **quailed**. He asked me if I meant to persist in my resistance. I told him I did, come what might; that he had used me like a brute for six months, and that I was determined to be used so no longer.	**Quailed:** weakened, became less	

13. With that, he **strove** to drag me to a stick that was lying just out of the stable door. He meant to knock me down. But just as he was leaning over to get the stick, I seized him with both hands by his collar, and brought him by a sudden snatch to the ground. By this time, Bill came. Covey called upon him for assistance. Bill wanted to know what he could do.	**Strove:** Bill came. Covey called upon him for assistance.	
Covey said, "Take hold of him, take hold of him!" Bill said his master hired him out to work, and not to help to whip me; so he left Covey and myself to fight our own battle out. We were at it for nearly two hours. Covey at length let me go, puffing and blowing at a great rate, saying that if I had not resisted, he would not have whipped me half so much. The truth was, that he had not whipped me at all. I considered him as getting entirely the worst end of the bargain; for he had drawn no blood from me, but I had from him. The whole six months afterwards that I spent with Mr. Covey, he never laid the weight of his finger upon me in anger. He would occasionally say he didn't want to get hold of me again. "No," thought I, "you need not; for you will come off worse than you did before."	15. What does Bill do that helps Douglass? 16. How does the fight end? 17. Why doesn't Covey try to whip Douglass again? Covey and myself to fight our battle out.	10. Why does Douglass describe Covey as "puffing and blowing at a great rate?" he thinks that Covey don't do anything and that he is weak
14. This battle with Mr. Covey was the turning-point in my career as a slave. It **rekindled** the few **expiring embers** of freedom, and **revived** within me a sense of my own manhood. It recalled the departed self-confidence, and inspired me again with a determination to be free. The **gratification** afforded by the **triumph** was a full **compensation** for whatever else might follow, even death itself. He only can understand the deep satisfaction which I experienced, who has himself **repelled** by force the bloody arm of slavery. I felt as I never felt before. It was a glorious **resurrection**, from the tomb of slavery, to the heaven of freedom. My long-crushed spirit rose, cowardice departed, bold defiance took its place; and I now resolved that, however long I might remain a slave in form, the day had passed forever when I could be a slave in fact. I did not hesitate to let it	**Rekindled:** **Expiring embers:** the last coals of a fire, just going out **Revived:** **Gratification:** pleasure, satisfaction **Triumph:** victory **Compensation:** payment **Repelled:** **Resurrection:** rebirth	11. Why does Douglass refer to the fight as a "resurrection"?" To what is he alluding? Why would this appeal to his audience? "I now resolved that, however long I might remain a slave in form, the day had passed forever when I could be a slave in fact."

be known of me, that the white man who expected to succeed in whipping, must also succeed in killing me.	18. Why was the fight with Covey important for Douglass?	12. What does that mean? How does the rest of the paragraph support it?
15. From this time I was never again what might be called fairly whipped, though I remained a slave four years afterwards. I had several fights, but was never whipped.		

Whole Excerpt

PURPOSE: How does this excerpt support the two positions Douglass held about slavery that are listed below?

1. Slavery is terrible for slaves.

___

___

___

2. Slavery corrupts slaveholders.

___

___

___

EXPEDITIONARY
LEARNING

Complete Sentences Practice

I. Identifying Sentence Fragments

Name: ______________________________

Date: ______________________________

Directions: Read the sentences below. Circle the ones that are not complete sentences.

1. Ben forgot his sunscreen.
2. Shifting into warp speed.
3. Lions are scary animals.
4. If you say that one more time.
5. Walking around the lake.
6. Karen and Ann are proud of the magazine.
7. Because Suzanne likes to ride horses.
8. He ordered a cheese pizza.
9. Sleeps in a bed.
10. When Brent fakes out the point guard.

Directions: Choose three of the options that were not complete sentences. Rewrite them here to make them into complete sentences. You will need to add words.

1.

2.

3.

II. Identifying Run-on Sentences

Name: ______________________________

Date: ______________________________

Directions: Read the sentences below. Circle the ones that are run-on sentences.

1. Ben forgot his sunscreen, and he got a sunburn.
2. Lions are scary animals, they can kill people.
3. While they were walking around the lake, they saw six ducks.
4. Because he was hungry, he ordered a cheese pizza.
5. He ordered a cheese pizza, when it came he ate all of it.
6. Brent fakes the point guard out, he shoots a basket, he scores the winning points for his team.

Directions: Now choose three of the above that were not complete sentences. Rewrite them below to make them into complete sentences. You may need to change, delete, or add words and/or punctuation.

1.

2.

3.

Mid-Unit Assessment, Part 1

Analyzing Storyteller's Craft

Comparing Written and Oral Stories

Name: ____

Date: ____

Harriet Tubman

by Eloise Greenfield

Harriet Tubman didn't take no stuff
Wasn't scared of nothing neither
Didn't come in this world to be no slave
And wasn't going to stay one either
"Farewell!" she sang to her friends one night
She was mighty sad to leave 'em
But she ran away that dark, hot night
Ran looking for her freedom
She ran to the woods and she ran through the woods
With the slave catchers right behind her
And she kept on going till she got to the North
Where those mean men couldn't find her
Nineteen times she went back South
To get three hundred others
She ran for her freedom nineteen times
To save Black sisters and brothers
Harriet Tubman didn't take no stuff
Wasn't scared of nothing neither
Didn't come in this world to be no slave
And didn't stay one either
And didn't stay one either

Directions

1. **Read the poem silently** as your teacher reads it aloud.
2. **Watch the video** of Thelma Thomas performing this poem.

3. **Reflect** on which parts of the poem were emphasized. **Circle five phrases** that you remember Mrs. Thomas emphasizing.
4. **Analyze the performance.** Watch the video of Mrs. Thomas performing the poem again. This time, take note in the margins of the way she uses her voice and body to emphasize important phrases and reinforce meaning.
5. **Read through the questions** on the assessment.
6. **Watch the video again**, as needed.
7. **Write your ideas:** Complete the written part of the assessment.

Analysis

1. Choose two of the lines you remember and explain what tools Mrs. Thomas uses to make you remember them. (RL.7.7)

___

___

___

2. This poem is about a strong woman. Explain two ways Mrs. Thomas uses the tools in the Storyteller's Toolbox to reflect on the strength of Harriet Tubman. (RL.7.7)

___

___

___

3. This storyteller decided to repeat these lines four times instead of three. She also sings them. Why would the storyteller emphasize these lines more than any other lines in the poem? (RL.7.1, RL.7.7)

Harriet Tubman didn't take no stuff
Wasn't scared of nothing neither
Didn't come in this world to be no slave
And didn't stay one either

___

___

___

Analysis Note-Catcher (Excerpt 4)

Name: ______________________________

Date: ______________________________

Chapter 10, Paragraphs 1–3, 5, 6, 10–13

What does Douglass say? **What is this excerpt about?**	**(See narrative arc on the next page)**	
Position: Why does he say it? (Briefly explain the connection between this excerpt and each of the two positions listed below.)	**Evidence:** What words, phrases, and sentences show his position? (Choose one or two quotes for each position; give the source and briefly state what each refers to.)	**Analysis:** What is the position that Douglass is trying to disprove? How does this quote prove that this position is incorrect?
Slavery corrupts slave owners.		
Slavery was terrible for slaves.		

Narrative Arc

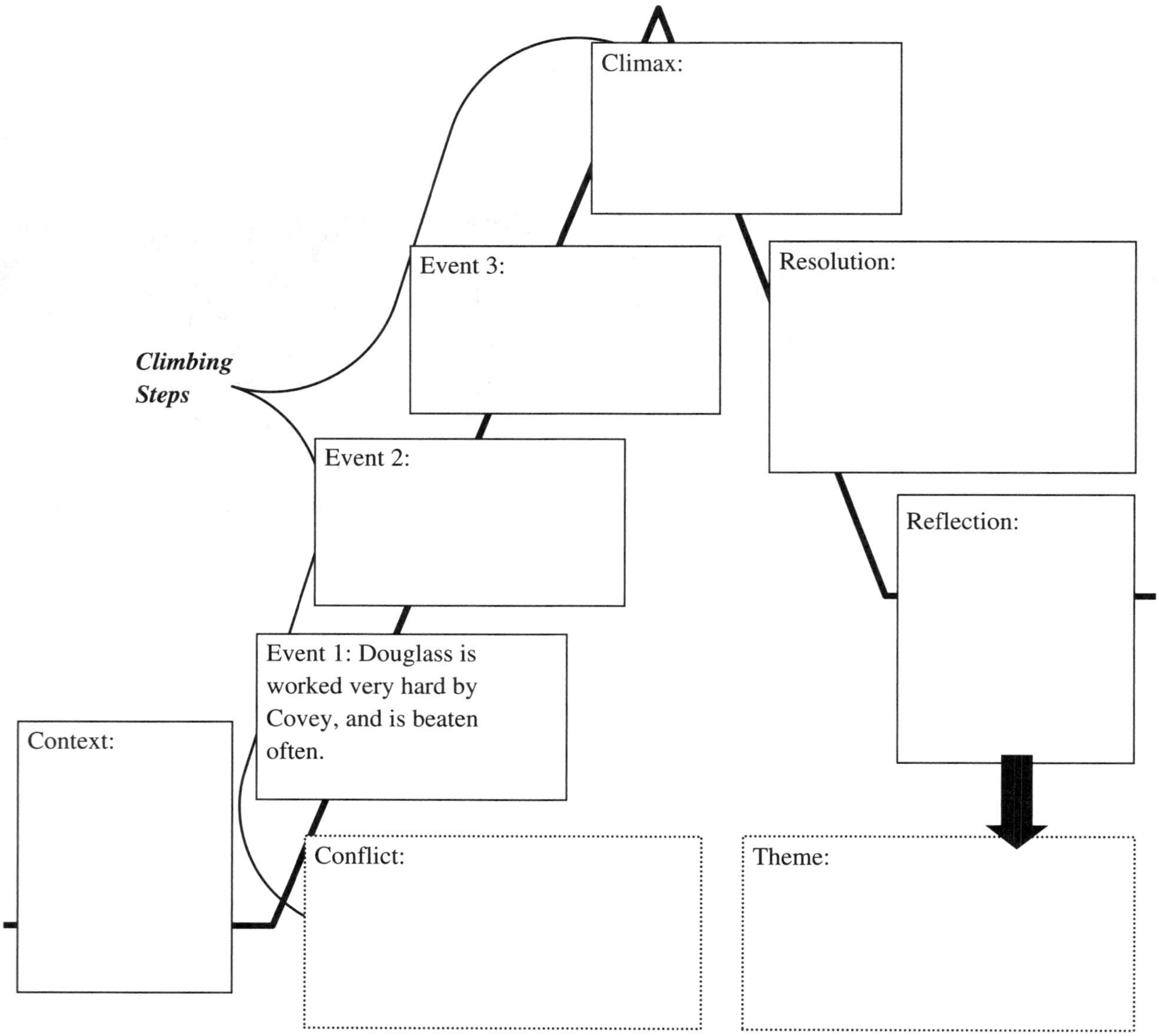

Climax:

Event 3:

Resolution:

Climbing Steps

Event 2:

Reflection:

Event 1: Douglass is worked very hard by Covey, and is beaten often.

Context:

Conflict:

Theme:

EXPEDITIONARY
LEARNING

Constructed Response (Excerpt 4)

"The Fight with Covey"

Name: ______________________________

Date: ______________________________

Directions: Reread Excerpt 4 from *Narrative of the Life of Frederick Douglass*. Answer the following questions in at least one paragraph: "How did Frederick Douglass's life change as a result of the fight with Covey? How did his life not change as a result of the fight with Covey? What specific examples from the text support your thinking?"

Reminders:

- Recycle the prompt.
- Give detailed examples from the text.
- Answer all parts of the question.
- Write in complete sentences.

Text and Questions (Excerpt 5)

"An Escape Attempt"

Narrative of the Life of Frederick Douglass

Source: Douglass, Frederick. Narrative of the Life of Frederick Douglass. *Boston, Massachusetts: Anti-Slavery Office, 1845. Project Gutenberg.*

Name: ____

Date: ____

Chapter 10, Paragraphs 26–31, 33–37, and 40

Background: In January 1834, Frederick Douglass leaves Covey and begins living on Mr. Freeland's plantation. Mr. Freeland is a slaveholder who is less cruel and more tolerable than the previous one. Douglass starts a Sabbath School, where he teaches at least 40 fellow slaves how to read. Slaveholders shut the school down. Douglass begins the year 1835 with a burning desire to escape to freedom in the North.

Text	Second Read Questions	Third Read Questions
1. At the close of the year 1834, Mr. Freeland again hired me of my master, for the year 1835. But, by this time, I began to want to live *upon free land* as well as *with Freeland*; and I was no longer content, therefore, to live with him or any other slaveholder . . . I was fast approaching manhood, and year after year had passed, and I was still a slave. These thoughts roused me—I must do something. I therefore resolved that 1835 should not pass without witnessing an attempt, on my part, to secure my liberty. But I was not willing to **cherish** this determination alone. My fellow-slaves [many of whom he had taught in Sabbath school] were dear to me. I was anxious to have them participate with me in this, my life-giving determination. I therefore, though with great **prudence**, commenced early to **ascertain** their views and feelings in regard to their condition, and to **imbue** their minds with thoughts of freedom . . . I went first to Henry, next to John, then to the others. I found, in them all, warm hearts and noble spirits. They were ready to hear, and ready to act when a **feasible** plan should be proposed. This was what I wanted. We met often, and consulted frequently, and told our hopes and fears, **recounted** the difficulties, real and imagined, which we should be called on to meet. At times we were almost **disposed** to give up, and try to content ourselves with our wretched lot; at others, we were firm and unbending in our determination to go.	1. What does Douglass decide he will do in 1834? **Cherish:** to keep or take care of something or someone you hold dear **Prudence:** caution **Ascertain:** figure out **Imbue:** 2. *Feasible* is from the root *fais*, which means do or make. The suffix is *-able*. Given that, what do you think *feasible* means? 3. *Recounted* has the prefix *re-*, which means again. What does Douglass do again in this paragraph? **Disposed:**	1. Given some of Douglass's concerns about escaping to freedom, what do you think may have prevented other slaves in the 1800s from attempting to escape from slavery? Use examples from the text.

Whenever we suggested any plan, there was shrinking—the odds were fearful. Our path was beset with the greatest obstacles; and if we succeeded in **gaining the end** of it, our right to be free was yet questionable—we were yet liable to be returned to **bondage**. We could see no spot, this side of the ocean, where we could be free.	**Gaining the end:** reaching the goal **Bondage:**	
We knew nothing about Canada. Our knowledge of the north did not extend farther than New York; and to go there, and be forever harassed with the frightful liability of being returned to slavery—with the certainty of being treated tenfold worse than before—the thought was truly a horrible one, and one which it was not easy to overcome. The case sometimes stood thus: At every gate through which we were to pass, we saw a watchman—at every ferry a guard—on every bridge a **sentinel**—and in every wood a patrol. We were **hemmed in** upon every side. Here were the difficulties, real or imagined—the good to be sought, and the evil to be **shunned**.	4. Underline two of Douglass's concerns about trying to escape from slavery. **Sentinel:** a soldier or guard whose job is to stand and keep watch **Hemmed in:** **Shunned:** deliberately avoided someone or something	2. What is Douglass describing when he writes, "its robes already crimsoned with the blood of millions, and even now feasting itself greedily upon our own flesh"? What type of figurative language is Douglass using here in this quote? a. Simile b. Metaphor c. Allusion d. Personification How does this help him make his point?
On the one hand, there stood slavery, a stern reality, glaring frightfully upon us,—its robes already crimsoned with the blood of millions, and even now feasting itself greedily upon our own flesh. On the other hand, away back in the dim distance, under the flickering light of the north star, behind some craggy hill or snow-covered mountain, stood a doubtful freedom—half frozen—beckoning us to come and share its hospitality.		

<table>
<tr>
<td>2. In coming to a fixed determination to run away, we did more than Patrick Henry, when he resolved upon liberty or death. With us it was a doubtful liberty at most, and almost certain death if we failed. For my part, I should prefer death to hopeless bondage.</td>
<td>5. Patrick Henry, a delegate from Virginia who was trying to get his state to join the Revolutionary War, wrote a speech where he said, "Give me liberty or give me death!"
What type of figurative language does Douglass use when he mentions Patrick Henry and his own "doubtful liberty at most, and almost certain death"?
a. Simile
b. Juxtaposition
c. Allusion
d. Vivid word choice</td>
<td>3. Why does Douglass so clearly explain the dangers of trying to escape? How does it convey his position about slavery?</td>
</tr>
<tr>
<td>3. The plan we finally concluded upon was, to get a large canoe belonging to Mr. Hamilton, and upon the Saturday night previous to Easter holidays, paddle directly up the Chesapeake Bay. On our arrival at the head of the bay, a distance of seventy or eighty miles from where we lived, it was our purpose to turn our canoe adrift, and follow the guidance of the north star till we got beyond the limits of Maryland. Our reason for taking the water route was, that we were less liable to be suspected as runaways; we hoped to be regarded as fishermen; whereas, if we should take the land route, we should be subjected to interruptions of almost every kind. Any one having a white face, and being so disposed, could stop us, and subject us to examination.</td>
<td>Purpose:
Adrift: not fastened to anything; a boat that is adrift will float away
Liable:
Subjected to:
6. What was the escape plan?</td>
<td></td>
</tr>
</table>

<table>
<tr>
<td>4. The week before our intended start, I wrote several protections, one for each of us. As well as I can remember, they were in the following words, to wit:—

"This is to certify that I, the undersigned, have given the bearer, my servant, full liberty to go to Baltimore, and spend the Easter holidays. Written with mine own hand, &c., 1835.

WILLIAM HAMILTON

Near St. Michael's, in Talbot county, Maryland."

We were not going to Baltimore; but, in going up the bay, we went toward Baltimore, and these protections were only intended to protect us while on the bay.</td>
<td>7. What is a protection? How would it help Douglass and the other escaping slaves?</td>
<td></td>
</tr>
<tr>
<td>5. After a painful waiting, the Saturday morning, whose night was to witness our departure, came. I hailed it with joy, bring what of sadness it might. Friday night was a sleepless one for me. I probably felt more anxious than the rest, because I was, by common consent, at the head of the whole affair. The responsibility of success or failure lay heavily upon me. The glory of the one, and the confusion of the other, were alike mine. The first two hours of that morning were such as I never experienced before, and hope never to again. Early in the morning, we went, as usual, to the field. We were spreading manure; and all at once, while thus engaged, I was overwhelmed with an indescribable feeling, in the fullness of which I turned to Sandy, who was near by, and said, "We are betrayed!" "Well," said he, "that thought has this moment struck me." We said no more. I was never more certain of any thing.</td>
<td>8. What does Douglass mean when he says, "We are betrayed!"? What has happened to their plan to escape?</td>
<td></td>
</tr>
</table>

EXPEDITIONARY LEARNING

6. The horn was blown as usual, and we went up from the field to the house for breakfast. I went for the form, more than for want of any thing to eat that morning. Just as I got to the house, in looking out at the lane gate, I saw four white men, with two colored men. Mr. Freeland put his head in at the door, and called me by name, saying, there were some gentlemen at the door who wished to see me. I stepped to the door, and inquired what they wanted. They at once seized me, and, without giving me any **satisfaction**, tied me—**lashing** my hands closely together. I insisted upon knowing what the matter was. They at length said, that they had learned I had been in a "scrape," and that I was to be examined before my master; and if their information proved false, I should not be hurt.	**Satisfaction:** reason 9. What set of context clues helps you figure out what *lash* means? a. seize, tied, hands closely together b. satisfaction, inquired, hands c. at once, tied, without d. tied, insisted, scrape	
7. In a few moments, they succeeded in tying John. They then turned to Henry, who had by this time returned, and commanded him to cross his hands. "I won't!" said Henry, in a firm tone, indicating his readiness to meet the consequences of his refusal. "Won't you?" said Tom Graham, the constable. "No, I won't!" said Henry, in a still stronger tone. With this, two of the constables pulled out their shining pistols, and swore, by their Creator, that they would make him cross his hands or kill him. Each cocked his pistol, and, with fingers on the trigger, walked up to Henry, saying, at the same time, if he did not cross his hands, they would blow his damned heart out. "Shoot me, shoot me!" said Henry; "you can't kill me but once. Shoot, shoot—and be damned! *I won't be tied!*"	10. What does Henry refuse to do? Why?	4. What details does Douglass give to convey Henry's bravery? Why does he make sure his audience sees Henry as brave?

This he said in a tone of loud **defiance**; and at the same time, with a motion as quick as lightning, he with one single stroke dashed the pistols from the hand of each constable. As he did this, all hands fell upon him, and, after beating him some time, they finally overpowered him, and got him tied.	11. "This he said in a tone of loud defiance; and at the same time, with a motion as quick as lightning, he with one single stroke dashed the pistols from the hand of each constable." What does *defiance* mean in this sentence? a. Behavior that shows you are unhappy with someone b. Behavior that shows you are angry with someone c. Behavior that shows you refuse to do what someone tells you to do, especially because you do not respect them d. Behavior that shows you are moving quickly	
8. During the scuffle, I managed, I know not how, to get my pass out, and, without being discovered, put it into the fire. We were all now tied . . . Just a moment previous to the scuffle with Henry, Mr. Hamilton suggested the **propriety** of making a search for the protections which	**Propriety:** recommended action or behavior 12. Why were Douglass and his friends "not yet convicted on the intention to run away"?	

he had understood Frederick had written for himself and the rest. But, just at the moment he was about carrying his proposal into effect, his aid was needed in helping to tie Henry; and the excitement attending the scuffle caused them either to forget, or to deem it unsafe, under the circumstances, to search. So we were not yet convicted of the intention to run away.		
9. When we got about half way to St. Michael's, while the constables having us in charge were looking ahead, Henry inquired of me what he should do with his pass. I told him to eat it with his biscuit, and own nothing; and we passed the word around, "Own nothing"; and "Own nothing!" said we all. Our confidence in each other was unshaken.	13. What does Douglass mean by "own nothing" and why do Douglass, Henry, and John repeat those words?	
10. I was now left to my fate. I was all alone, and within the walls of a stone prison. But a few days before, and I was full of hope. I expected to have been safe in a land of freedom; but now I was covered with gloom, sunk down to the utmost despair. I thought the possibility of freedom was gone. I was kept in this way about one week, at the end of which, Captain Auld, my master, to my surprise and **utter** astonishment, came up, and took me out, with the intention of sending me, with a gentleman of his acquaintance, into Alabama. But, from some cause or other, he did not send me to Alabama, but concluded to send me back to Baltimore, to live again with his brother Hugh, and to **learn a trade**.	14. Where do the constables take Douglass? **Utter:** **Learn a trade:** to learn to do a particular craft, such as making clocks or boats, or weaving cloth	5. How does Douglass's mood change from the beginning of the excerpt to the end? Provide several examples to support your idea.

Whole Excerpt

PURPOSE: How does this excerpt support the two positions Douglass held about slavery that are listed below?

1. Slavery is terrible for slaves.

   ____

2. Slavery corrupts slaveholders.

   ____

EXPEDITIONARY LEARNING

Figurative Language Matching Game Cards

Note: This sheet, with the sentence strips and tool cards aligned in this way, can serve as an answer key. Be aware that some sentence strips could be both a specific device and vivid word choice.

Sentence Strips	Tool Cards
This he said in a tone of loud defiance; and at the same time, with a motion as quick as lightning, he with one single stroke dashed the pistols from the hand of each constable. (Excerpt 5, Par. 7)	Simile
"There stood slavery, a stern reality, glaring frightfully upon us." (Excerpt 5, Par. 1)	Personification
"Its robes already crimsoned with the blood of millions, and even now feasting itself greedily upon our own flesh." (Excerpt 5, Par. 1)	Personification
"Now I was covered with gloom, sunk down to the utmost despair." (Par. 10)	Vivid Word Choice
"I was seized with a violent aching of the head, attended with extreme dizziness; I trembled in every limb." (Excerpt 4, Par. 7)	Vivid Word Choice
"The dark night of slavery closed in upon me; and behold a man transformed into a brute!" (Excerpt 4, Par. 4)	Metaphor
"Here were the difficulties, real or imagined—the good to be sought, and the evil to be shunned." (Excerpt 5, Par. 1)	Juxtaposition
"In coming to a fixed determination to run away, we did more than Patrick Henry, when he resolved upon liberty or death. With us it was a doubtful liberty at most, and almost certain death if we failed." (Excerpt 5, Par. 4)	Allusion
"The responsibility of success or failure lay heavily upon me. The glory of the one, and the confusion of the other, were alike mine." (Excerpt 5, Par. 5)	Juxtaposition
"It was a glorious resurrection, from the tomb of slavery, to the heaven of freedom." (Excerpt 4, Par. 14)	Metaphor

EXPEDITIONARY
LEARNING

Figurative Language Matching Game Directions

1. Read the cards and clarify any vocabulary.
2. Walk around and find a match: A tool card needs to be matched with a sentence strip, which has an example of that tool from the *Narrative.*
3. Sit down together once a match is made.
4. Discuss the example and tool. Talk about why Douglass used that particular tool.

Figurative Language Card Directions

Directions

- Skim Excerpt 4 and Excerpt 5.
- Choose an example of figurative language that you find effective.
- Fill out a Vivid Word Choice Card.

Card Prompt	**Figurative Language Card**
	Name:____________________ Write the sentence or part of the sentence; underline the word(s) you are focusing on. Type of figurative language: Effect on meaning/tone:

Card Example:	**Figurative Language Card**
	Name:____________________ Write the sentence or part of the sentence; underline the word(s) you are focusing on. *"His comings were <u>like a thief in the night</u>." (Excerpt 4, Paragraph 3)* Type of figurative language: *Simile* Effect on meaning/tone: *Douglass is describing how Covey always snuck up on slaves to make sure they were working. By comparing him to a thief, Douglass adds to the suggestion that Covey was an evil and immoral person.*

Figurative Language Cards

Figurative Language Card

Name:

Write the sentence or part of the sentence; underline the phrase you are focusing on.

Type of figurative language:

Effect on meaning/tone:

Figurative Language Card

Name:

Write the sentence or part of the sentence; underline the phrase you are focusing on.

Type of figurative language:

Effect on meaning/tone:

Figurative Language Card

Name:

Write the sentence or part of the sentence; underline the phrase you are focusing on.

Type of figurative language:

Effect on meaning/tone:

Analysis Note-Catcher (Excerpt 5)

"An Escape Attempt"

Narrative of the Life of Frederick Douglass

Name: ____

Date: ____

Chapter 10, Paragraphs 26 –31, 33–37, and 40

What does Douglass say? **What is this excerpt about?**	**(See narrative arc on the next page)**	
Position: Why does he say it? Briefly explain the connection between this excerpt and each of the two positions listed here.	**Evidence:** What words, phrases, and sentences show his position? (Choose one or two quotes for each position; give the source and briefly state what each refers to.)	**Analysis:** What is the position that Douglass is trying to disprove? How does this quote prove that this position is incorrect?
Slavery corrupts slave owners.		
Slavery was terrible for slaves.		

Narrative Arc

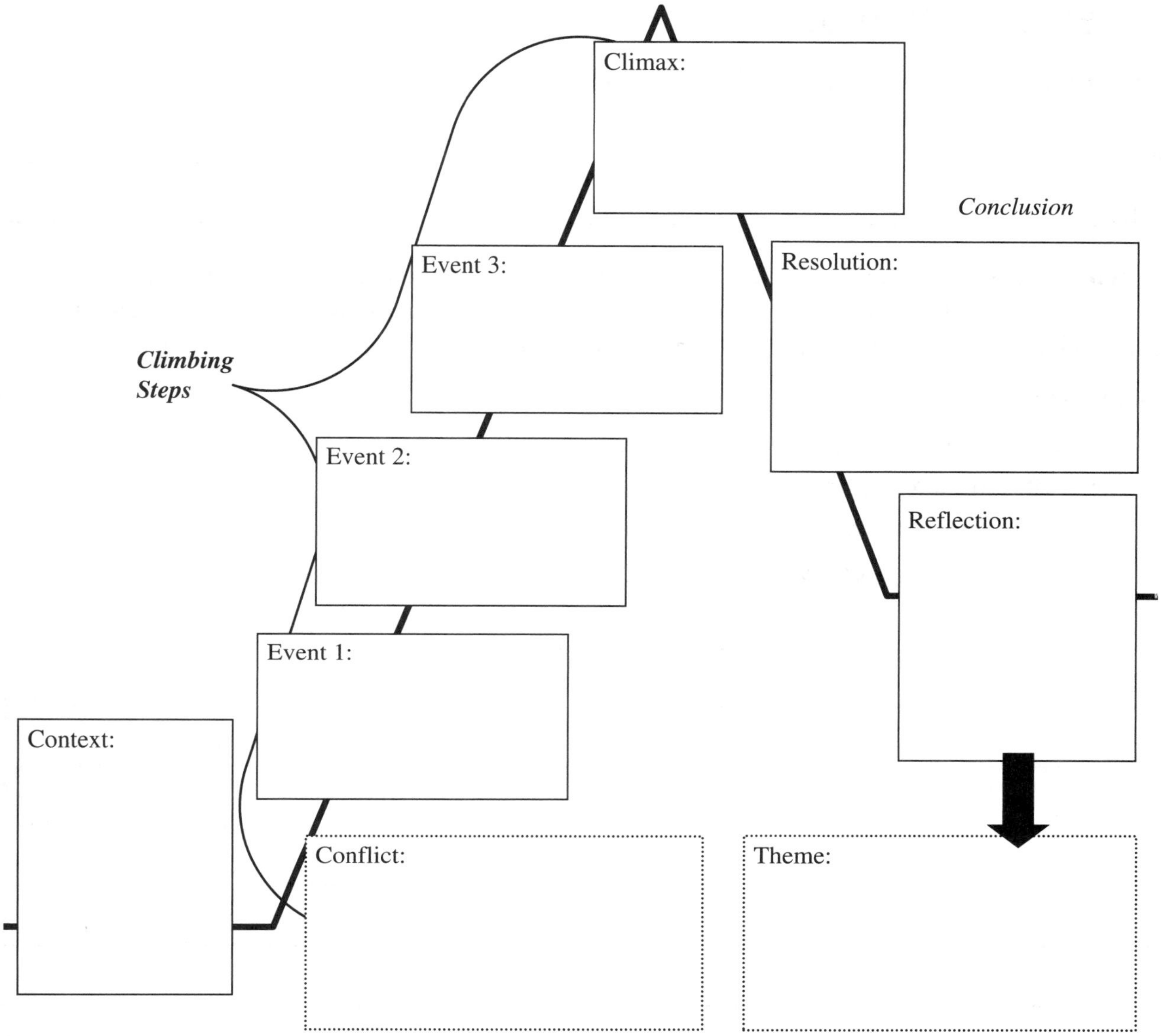

Climax:

Conclusion

Event 3:

Resolution:

Climbing Steps

Event 2:

Reflection:

Event 1:

Context:

Conflict:

Theme:

EXPEDITIONARY
LEARNING

Constructed Response (Excerpt 5)

"An Escape Attempt"

Narrative of the Life of Frederick Douglass

Name: ____

Date: ____

Directions: Reread Excerpt 5 from *Narrative of the Life of Frederick Douglass*. Answer the questions: "How does Frederick Douglass show leadership in this excerpt? What motivates him to take on these leadership roles? What specific examples from the text support your thinking?"

Reminders:

- Recycle the prompt.
- Give detailed examples from the text.
- Answer all parts of the question.
- Write in complete sentences.

____

____

____

____

____

____

____

____

____

____

____

____

____

Mid-Unit Assessment, Part 2: Analyzing Author's Craft

Analyzing Purpose and Craft in Douglass's *Narrative*

Name: Darion Bell

Date: 2/27/2019

Directions: Read the following selection from *Narrative of the Life of Frederick Douglass* and answer the questions below. Feel free to take gist notes in the margin to help you understand what you read.

it said slaveholder's it was their base ingratitude to my poor old grandmother

1	Very soon after my return to Baltimore, my mistress, Lucretia, died, leaving her husband and one child, Amanda; and in a very short time after her death, Master Andrew died. Now all the property of my old master, slaves included, was in the hands of strangers,—strangers who had had nothing to do with accumulating it. Not a slave was left free. All remained slaves, from the youngest to the oldest. If any one thing in my experience, more than another, served to deepen my conviction of the **infernal** character of slavery, and to fill me with unutterable **loathing** of slaveholders, it was their **base** ingratitude to my poor old grandmother.	**Infernal:** evil **Loathing:** strong hatred **Base:** without moral principles
2	She had served my old master faithfully from youth to old age. She had been the source of all his wealth; she had peopled his plantation with slaves; she had become a great-grandmother in his service. She had rocked him in infancy, attended him in childhood, served him through life, and at his death wiped from his icy brow the cold death sweat, and closed his eyes forever. She was nevertheless left a slave—a slave for life—a slave in the hands of strangers; and in their hands she saw her children, her grandchildren, and her great-grandchildren, divided, like so many sheep, without being gratified with the small privilege of a single word, as to their or her own destiny. And, to cap the climax of their base ingratitude and **fiendish barbarity**, my grandmother, who was now very old, having outlived my old master and all his children, having seen the beginning and end of all of them, and her present owners finding she was of but little value, her frame already racked with the pains of old age, and complete helplessness fast stealing over her once active limbs, they took her to the woods, built her a little hut, put up a little mud-chimney, and then made her welcome to the privilege of supporting herself there in perfect loneliness; thus virtually turning her out to die! If my poor old grandmother now lives, she lives to suffer in utter loneliness; she lives to remember and **mourn** over the loss of children, the loss of grandchildren, and the loss of great-grandchildren.	**Fiendish barbarity:** evil, cruel act

<table>
<tr><td>3</td><td>They are, in the language of the slave's poet, Whittier,—

"Gone, gone, sold and gone
To the rice swamp dank and lone,
Where the slave-whip ceaseless swings,
Where the noisome insect stings,
Where the fever-demon strews
Poison with the falling dews,
Where the sickly sunbeams glare
Through the hot and misty air:—
Gone, gone, sold and gone
To the rice swamp dank and lone,
From Virginia hills and waters—
Woe is me, my stolen daughters!"</td><td></td></tr>
<tr><td>4</td><td>The hearth is desolate. The children, the unconscious children, who once sang and danced in her presence, are gone. She gropes her way, in the darkness of age, for a drink of water. Instead of the voices of her children, she hears by day the moans of the dove, and by night the screams of the hideous owl. All is gloom. The grave is at the door. And now, when weighed down by the pains and aches of old age, when the head inclines to the feet, when the beginning and ending of human existence meet, and helpless infancy and painful old age combine together—at this time, this most needful time, the time for the exercise of that tenderness and affection which children only can exercise towards a declining parent—my poor old grandmother, the devoted mother of twelve children, is left all alone, in yonder little hut, before a few dim embers. She stands—she sits—she staggers—she falls—she groans—she dies—and there are none of her children or grandchildren present, to wipe from her wrinkled brow the cold sweat of death, or to place beneath the sod her fallen remains. Will not a righteous God visit for these things?</td><td>Hearth: the area by the fireplace; also used to mean the home in general
Unconscious: unable to realize what is going on
In this case the children don't know how bad their grandmother's life is because they aren't there.</td></tr>
</table>

Source: Douglass, Frederick. Narrative of the Life of Frederick Douglass. *Boston, Massachusetts: Anti-Slavery Office, 1845. Project Gutenberg.*

EXPEDITIONARY LEARNING

Mid-Unit Assessment, Part 2: Analyzing Stories

Analyzing Purpose and Craft in Douglass's *Narrative*

Name: Darion Ben

Date: 2/27/2019

Questions

1. What happened to the grandmother of Frederick Douglass? (RI.7.2)

She was a slave and douglass did not want that and she died of working as a slave

2. Douglass juxtaposes how his grandmother should be treated with how she is treated. Please fill out this chart with text-based evidence. (RI.7.1)

What should happen to her	What is happening to her
She should have children dancing in her presence	The children the unconscious children who once sang and danced in her presence.
Hearing the voice of her children	instead of the voices of her children she hears by day the moans of the dove.
Needs children to physically help her	She need help

3. Does Douglass believe that his grandmother deserved what happened to her? Why or why not? What are two pieces of evidence that he gives to support his claim? (RI.7.1)

No She stands - she sits - She staggers - She falls - she groans - She dies.

4. In Paragraph 1 Frederick Douglass hints at his purpose for recounting what happened to his grandmother. Choose one and support it with evidence. (RI.7.6)
   A. His purpose is to convince his audience that slavery is terrible for slaves.
   B. His purpose is to convince his audience that slavery corrupts white slave owners.

Position	Evidence	Analysis of Evidence

5. Reread Paragraph 3. Then circle five phrases that create a mood for the hut where his grandmother lives. Describe the mood that these phrases create. (RI.7.4, L.7.5b)

   How does the mood of the hut reinforce what happened to his grandmother?

6. Read the following sentence from Paragraph 2. (L.7.5b)

   "She was nevertheless left a slave—a slave for life—a slave in the hands of strangers; and in their hands she saw her children, her grandchildren, and her great-grandchildren, divided, like so many sheep, without being gratified with the small privilege of a single word, as to their or her own destiny."

   What figurative language does Douglass use to make a comparison in this sentence?

   How does this comparison reinforce the slave owner's attitude toward the slaves?

7. Reread this sentence from Paragraph 2. (L.7.5c)

   "If my poor old grandmother now lives, she lives to suffer in utter loneliness; she lives to remember and **mourn** over the loss of children, the loss of grandchildren, and the loss of great-grandchildren."

   What does *mourn* mean in this sentence?

   A. To be angry
   B. To be sad
   C. To be confused
   D. To be heartbroken

8. Read the following sentence from the last paragraph.

   "She stands—she sits—she staggers—she falls—she groans—she dies—and there are none of her children or grandchildren present, to wipe from her wrinkled brow the cold sweat of death, or to place beneath the **sod** her fallen remains."

   Choose a group of context clues that best helps you determine the meaning of the word *sod.* (L.7.4a)

   A. she dies, place beneath, cold sweat of death
   B. she stands, cold sweat, grandchildren

C. she staggers, she falls, wrinkled brow

D. she groans, none of her children present, to wipe

9. Why does the word *stagger* come before the word *fall* in the sentence? How does this help you determine the meaning of *stagger*? (L.7.5b)

10. In Paragraph 3, Douglass uses the word *desolate,* which has the root *sole,* which means alone. What does Douglass mean when he describes his grandmother's hearth (or home) as desolate? (L.7.4b)

11. Reread this selection from Paragraph 4. Pay particular attention to the underlined words. (L.7.5b, L.7.4a and b)

"And now, when weighed down by the pains and aches of old age, when the head inclines to the feet, when the beginning and ending of human existence meet, and helpless infancy and painful old age combine together—at this time, this most needful time, the time for the exercise of that tenderness and affection which children only can exercise towards a declining parent—my poor old grandmother, the devoted mother of twelve children, is left all alone, in yonder little hut, before a few dim embers."

Frederick Douglass describes his grandmother's condition by saying she has both the helplessness of infancy and the pain of old age. This seems like a contradiction. What does this pairing of antonyms add to the reader's understanding of old age?

Why is old age a "needful" time?

EXPEDITIONARY
LEARNING

Entry Task

Predicting the Conclusion

Name: ______________________________

Date: ______________________________

What do you think happens at the end of Douglass's *Narrative*? Why do you think that?

____

____

____

____

____

____

____

____

EXPEDITIONARY LEARNING

Readers Theater

Narrative of the Life of Frederick Douglass Conclusion

Source: Adapted from Chapters 10 and 11, Narrative of the Life of Frederick Douglass.

Characters: Narrator, Frederick Douglass, Mr. Gardner, Workers 1–3, Master Hugh, Young Man

Script	Vocabulary
Narrator: A few weeks after Douglass went to Baltimore, Master Hugh hired him to Mr. William Gardner, a shipbuilder on Fell's Point.	
Mr. Gardner: "My workers will teach you how to **caulk,** so the planks on this ship don't leak water."	**Caulk:** to fill the holes or cracks in a ship with an oily or sticky substance in order to keep water out
Douglass: (nods head)	
Worker 1: "Fred, come help me to cant this timber here."	
Worker 2: "Fred, come carry this timber **yonder**."	**Yonder:** over there
Worker 3: "Fred, bring that roller here."	
Worker 1: "Fred, go get a fresh can of water."	
Worker 2: "Fred, come help saw off the end of this timber."	
(Douglass gets pulled in different directions by the workers.)	
Narrator: Douglass needed 12 hands to do all the work that was required, and no one taught him how to caulk properly.	
Mr. Gardner: "I hire black carpenters, most of whom are free, and whites to work alongside each other."	
Worker 1: (in angry voice) "We don't like that; they are threatening our jobs!"	
Worker 2: (in angry voice) "We are tired of it!"	
Worker 3: "Mr. Gardner, fire the black workers or else!"	

Mr. Gardner: "I will do no such thing!"	
(Workers attack Douglass.)	
Narrator: Douglass kept the vow he made after the fight with Mr. Covey, and struck back again, regardless of consequences; but they all came upon him, armed with sticks, stones, and heavy handspikes.	
(Douglass tries to fight back, but there are too many workers attacking.)	
Narrator: All this took place in sight of no fewer than 50 white ship carpenters, and not one **interposed** a friendly word; but some cried, "Kill him! Kill him! He struck a white person." Douglass's only chance for life was in flight. He succeeded in getting away without an additional blow.	**Interposed:** said something when other people were having a conversation or argument, interrupting them
Master Hugh: "You are never working for Mr. Gardner again; it is too dangerous! I will find someone to teach you how to caulk properly."	
Narrator: In the course of one year from the time he left Mr. Gardner's, Douglass commanded the highest wages given to the most experienced caulkers. He was bringing Master Hugh from six to seven dollars per week.	
Douglass: "Master Hugh, here are my weekly wages of six dollars."	
Master Hugh: (looks at Douglass fiercely) "Is this all? I want every last cent. Here, I suppose you can have six cents—keep working hard." (hands Douglass six cents)	
Narrator: The fact that Master Hugh gave Douglass any part of his wages was proof that he was **entitled** to the whole of them. In the spring of 1838, Douglass and Master Hugh came to new terms. Douglass was allowed the freedom to make all contracts with those for whom he worked, and find his own employment; and, in return for this liberty, he was to pay Hugh three dollars at the end of each week.	**Entitled:** the right to do or have something
Douglass (to audience): My board was two dollars and a half per week. This, with the wear and tear of clothing and caulking tools, made my regular expenses about six dollars per week. Master Hugh was still receiving all the benefits of slaveholding without its evils, while I endured all the evils of a slave, and suffered all the care and anxiety of a freeman. Whenever my condition is improved, it only increases my desire to be free.	

Narrator: During this part of Douglass's life, he planned, and succeeded in escaping from slavery. He cannot give you all the facts of his escape because it would **undoubtedly induce** greater **vigilance** on the part of slaveholders.	**Undoubtedly:** definitely true **Induce:** to persuade someone to do something that does not seem wise **Vigilance:** careful attention
Narrator: As the time for Douglass's escape drew near, he began to think of his beloved friends in Baltimore and the thought of being separated from them forever was painful beyond expression.	
Douglass (to audience): Besides the pain of separation, the dread of a failure exceeded what I had experienced at my first attempt. It was life and death. But I remained firm. On the third day of September 1838, I left my chains and succeeded in reaching New York. How I did so—what direction I traveled, and by what mode of **conveyance**—I must leave unexplained.	**Conveyance:** vehicle
Narrator: Shortly after moving to New York, Douglass moved to New Bedford where it was safer. He found employment in loading a sloop with oil. It was new, dirty, and hard work; but he went at it with a glad heart and a willing hand. He was now his own master. There was no Master Hugh standing ready to rob him of his money the moment he earned it.	
Young Man: (tries to hand Douglass the paper) "Would you like to take the *Liberator* to read?"	**Liberator:** someone who frees another person
Douglass: "Yes, but just having made my escape from slavery, I am unable to pay for it now. In a few weeks, I will subscribe to it."	
Narrator: The paper came, and he read it from week to week. The paper became Douglass's meat and drink. His soul was set all on fire. Its sympathy for his brethren in bonds, its **scathing denunciations** of slaveholders, and its faithful exposures of slavery sent a thrill of joy through his soul, such as he had never felt before!	**Scathing:** critical or severe **Denunciation:** a public statement criticizing someone

(Douglass looks excited as he reads the "Liberator")	
Douglass (to audience): I had not long been a reader of the *Liberator* before I really understood the measures and spirit of the antislavery reform. I took right hold of the cause. I never felt happier than when in an antislavery meeting. While attending an antislavery convention at Nantucket, on the 11th of August 1841, I felt strongly moved to speak, and was at the same time much urged to do so by Mr. William C. Coffin, a gentleman who had heard me speak in the colored people's meeting at New Bedford. It was a severe cross, and I took it up reluctantly. The truth was, I felt myself a slave, and the idea of speaking to white people weighed me down. I spoke but a few moments when I felt a degree of freedom, and said what I desired with considerable ease. From that time until now, I have been engaged in pleading the cause of my brethren—with what success, and with what devotion, I leave those acquainted with my labors to decide.	

Personal Reflection

Name: ______________________________

Date: ______________________________

Directions: Write a personal reflection on the *Narrative* that responds to the following prompts:

- "What 'pulled' you most about Douglass's story?"
- "Why is it important to read *Narrative of the Life of Frederick Douglass* in 2015, almost 200 years after it was written?"

Share your personal reflection with someone at home or with a teacher.

Signature:

Name:

Relationship to student:

EXPEDITIONARY LEARNING

Entry Task

Writer's Reflection

Name: ______________________________

Date: ______________________________

Directions: In a few days you will write an on-demand essay that reflects your understanding of *Narrative of the Life of Frederick Douglass*. Please read over your Writing Improvement Tracker from Modules 1 and 2 to help you focus on your strengths and weaknesses.

1. What has been one of your strengths in the previous essay assignments?

____

____

2. What have you struggled with in past essay assignments?

____

____

3. What is your is goal (look at Essay from Module 2, Question 4) for this essay assignment?

____

____

4. What other goal do you have for this essay assignment?

____

____

5. How can I help you accomplish these goals?

____

____

Read through this list of possible strategies to improve your writing:

- Revise my writing (or my planning) multiple times.
- Ask myself, "Does this make sense?"
- Look at other models.
- Read the necessary texts closely.
- Read other people's work.
- Talk through my ideas with an adult.
- Ask questions when I have them.
- Use quote sandwiches.
- Take a break and reread with fresh eyes.
- Have another student write the gist of my paragraphs and make sure they match what I thought they were.

Circle any strategies that you have used to improve your writing.

Star two that you would like to try this time.

EXPEDITIONARY LEARNING

Writer's Glossary

Narrative of the Life of Frederick Douglass

Name: ______________________________

Date: ______________________________

The words here are from Module 3, Unit 2, Lessons 13–16.

Word/Phrase	Definition
purpose	
position	
audience	
support	
Other new words you encountered:	

End-of-Unit Assessment Essay Prompt

Directions: Draw on your reading and notes to plan and write an essay that addresses the following prompt.

In his *Narrative,* Frederick Douglass explains his purpose is to throw "light on the American slave system." Which aspects of slavery does his narrative bring to light? How does his position differ from that of those who defended slavery? How does he use his story to support his position?

EXPEDITIONARY LEARNING

Model Essay

"Telling the Truth about Slavery"

Name: ______________________________

Date: ______________________________

After escaping from slavery in the 1830s, Frederick Douglass embarked on a quest to abolish slavery. He knew the best way to abolish slavery was to "shine a light" on aspects of slavery and to tell a story that people did not know, the story of being a slave. The people who read his story in *Narrative of the Life of Frederick Douglass* were Northerners who were either apathetic to slavery or supportive of slavery. Using his own experience, Douglass argues that slavery created an unnatural order in society, and that instead of civilizing slaves, it corrupted them. These positions opposed commonly held Northern beliefs, especially the beliefs of those who defended slavery. By telling a compelling story that also proved the negative effects of slavery, Douglass built a convincing case for the abolition of slavery.	What are the aspects of slavery? Star and underline the claim of the essay.
Defenders of slavery often argued that slavery supported a natural order in society, but Douglass argues that slavery disrupts the natural order because it destroys family relationships. He describes the dynamics of his own family, which were distorted by slavery. Douglass's father was, in fact, his white master. He goes on to explain that this was very common, and it created a situation in which a father, instead of caring for his child, would "sell his own children to human flesh-mongers" (Chapter 1). If he did not, the father would be compelled to "stand by and see one white son tie up his brother . . . and ply the gory lash to his naked back" (Chapter 1). Many Northerners believed fathers should care for their children and brothers should stand together, and the images of a father selling his own children and a brother whipping his brother horrified them. These examples help to convey Douglass's position that slavery destroys natural family relationships.	What is the focus of the first body paragraph? Circle examples.

Another common misconception held by Northerners who defended slavery was that slavery civilized the African people. In order to counter this belief, Douglass uses the annual holidays slaves got from their slaveholders as an example. Every year between Christmas and New Year's, slaves were allowed to have time off. However, slaveholders, instead of encouraging a slave to participate in uplifting activities, would "adopt various plans to make him drunk" (Chapter 10). One such plan was taking bets as to which slave could drink the most whiskey and in "this way succeed in getting whole multitudes to drink to excess" (Chapter 10). If slavery civilized slaves, then slaveholders would not intentionally try to make slaves drink too much. This example illustrates that slaveholders in fact encouraged slaves to be uncivilized and immoral. Northerners would have expected slaveholders to guide their slaves with fatherly tenderness into being morally upright, and Douglass shatters this belief.	What is the focus of the second body paragraph? Circle examples.
Douglass's *Narrative* became a truth-telling tool used to expose the barbarities of slavery. This tool was purposefully directed at Northerners, whom Douglass saw as potential allies in the fight against the corrupt institution. Douglass directly counters the misconceptions that Northerners had, particularly those who defended slavery, and shows how slavery destroyed the family unit and created a culture of drunk, immoral beings. Understanding the life of a slave through Douglass's *Narrative* challenges many of the arguments made by the supporters of slavery, and helped further Douglass's purpose of abolishing slavery.	Check the three parts of the prompt.

Linking the Prompt to the Essay

Name: ______________________________

Date: ______________________________

Directions: Read the introduction again, paying particular attention to where the author addresses the three parts of the prompt. Connect each box to the corresponding sentence in the introduction.

1	2	3
In his *Narrative*, Frederick Douglass explains his purpose is to throw "light on the American slave system." Which aspects of slavery does his narrative bring to light?	How does his position differ from that of those who defended slavery?	How does he use his story to support his position?

After escaping from slavery in the 1830s, Frederick Douglass embarked on a quest to abolish slavery. He knew the best way to abolish slavery was to "shine a light" on aspects of slavery and to tell a story that people did not know, the story of being a slave. The people who read his story in *Narrative of the Life of Frederick Douglass* were Northerners who were either apathetic to slavery or supportive of slavery. Using his own experience, Douglass argues that slavery created an unnatural order in society, and that instead of civilizing slaves, it corrupted them. These positions opposed commonly held Northern beliefs, especially the beliefs of those who defended slavery. By telling a compelling story that also proved the negative effects of slavery, Douglass built a convincing case for the abolition of slavery.

Now reread the first body paragraph looking for the sentences that address each part of the prompt. Put the number of each prompt box over the corresponding sentence in the first body paragraph.

If time permits, repeat for the second body paragraph.

Exit Ticket

Closely Reading the Prompt

Name: ______________________________

Date: ______________________________

Directions: Complete this task individually.

Prompt

In his *Narrative,* Frederick Douglass explains his purpose is to throw "light on the American slave system." Which aspects of slavery does his narrative bring to light? How does his position differ from that of those who defended slavery? How does he use his story to support his position?

1. Please circle the five words from the prompt above that you must keep in mind in order to successfully write this essay.

2. How is this essay similar to and different from the *argumentative* essay you wrote in Module 2?

____

____

3. How is this essay similar to and different from the *analysis* essay you wrote for Module 1?

____

____

4. Rewrite what you are going to do in this essay in your own words.

____

____

____

____

EXPEDITIONARY LEARNING

Entry Task

Combining Sentences

Name: ______________________________

Date: ______________________________

Directions: Combine the following sentences. Suggested conjunctions:

while	nor
even though	yet
but	although
after	in order
and	to
before	either . . . or
because	not only . . . but also,
so	since

1. Frederick Douglass argued that slaves were treated like property. Northerners believed slaves were treated like children.

____

____

____

____

2. Frederick Douglass gave multiple examples of overseers who were cruel and heartless. Covey was one of the worst.

____

____

____

____

EXPEDITIONARY LEARNING

Homework: Part A

Directions: Combine the following sentences as you did in the previous Entry Task.

1. Frederick Douglass saw firsthand the corrupting influence of slavery. Northerners believed that slavery was good for Southerners.

2. Douglass describes horrific beatings. He also describes deplorable living conditions.

Homework: Part B

Directions: Underline the conjunction, then rewrite the following as two complete sentences.

1. Even though Frederick Douglass was forbidden to learn to read by Mr. Auld, he found a way and was soon reading everything he could get his hands on.

2. Because of the dangers of running away, most slaves didn't dare do it.

Frederick Douglass Essay Planner

Name: ____________________

Date: ____________________

Directions: Thoughtfully fill out the essay planner. Remember, you needn't write in complete sentences (in fact, some boxes may be combined into one sentence) until you write your final essay. But you do need to thoroughly explain your ideas. The more you have written and planned, the easier it will be to write your essay.

Focusing Questions: In his *Narrative,* Frederick Douglass explains that his purpose is to throw "light on the American slave system." Which aspects of slavery does his narrative bring to light? How does his position differ from that of people who defended slavery? How does he use his story to support his position?

I. Introduction	
Begins with a hook to capture the reader's interest and attention	
Give the context of Frederick Douglass and his overall purpose	
Give the context of Douglass's audience	
Focusing statement: Name the two positions of Douglass's that the essay will focus on	

II. Body Paragraph 1	
Explain the position of people who defended slavery or Northerners who were supportive of or indifferent to slavery	People who defended slavery believed . . . Defenders of slavery claimed that . . . Many Northerners believed . . . A common misconception of Northerners was . . .
Explain Frederick Douglass's position	Douglass argues . . . But Douglass wanted them to understand . . .
Give evidence (in a Quote Sandwich)	
Give additional evidence (in a Quote Sandwich)	
Analysis of evidence: How does this prove Douglass's position?	This shows that . . . This example proves . . . This illustrates that . . .
How does Douglass's evidence disprove the position of those who defend slavery?	
Concluding sentence	

II. Body Paragraph 2	
Explain the position of people who defended slavery or Northerners who were supportive of or indifferent to slavery	People who defended slavery believed . . . Defenders of slavery claimed that . . . Many Northerners believed . . . A common misconception of Northerners was . . .
Explain Frederick Douglass's position	Douglass argues . . . But Douglass wanted them to understand . . .
Give evidence (in a Quote Sandwich)	
Give additional evidence (in a Quote Sandwich)	
Analysis of evidence: How does this prove Douglass's position?	This shows that . . . This example proves . . . This illustrates that . . .
How does Douglass's evidence disprove the position of those who defend slavery?	
Concluding sentence	

IV. Conclusion	
Restate Frederick Douglass's purpose	
Summarize Douglass's positions	
Explain how his positions disproved the positions of those who defended slavery	

EXPEDITIONARY
LEARNING

Quote Sandwich

Name: ______________________________

Date: ______________________________

A sandwich is made up of three parts—the bread on top, the filling in the middle, and the bread on the bottom. A Quote Sandwich is similar; it is how you use evidence in an analysis essay. First, you introduce a quote by telling your reader the background information they need to understand the quote. Then, you include the quote. Last, you explain how the quote supports your idea. Read this example of using a quote in an analysis essay, then take a look at the graphic:

Every year between Christmas and New Year's, slaves were allowed to have time off. However slaveholders, instead of encouraging a slave to participate in uplifting activities, would "adopt various plans to make him drunk" (Chapter 10). One such plan was taking bets as to which slave could drink the most whiskey and in "this way succeed in getting whole multitudes to drink to excess" (Chapter 10). If slavery civilized slaves, then slaveholders would not intentionally try to make slaves drink too much. This example illustrates that slaveholders, in fact, encouraged slaves to be uncivilized, and immoral.

Note: In your essays, you can just list the excerpt number that a quote is from.

Introduce the quote	**Example**
Introduce the quote with context—the background information your readers need to understand the quote.	*Every year between Christmas and New Year's, slaves were allowed to have time off.*
Include the quote	**Example**
Make sure it is punctuated correctly and if possible, integrated smoothly into a sentence. Be sure to include a citation (tell the excerpt number a quote is from). Notice that the start of the sentence gives context that helps the reader understand the actual quote.	*However, slaveholders, instead of encouraging a slave to participate in uplifting activities, would "adopt various plans to make him drunk" (Excerpt ____). One such plan was taking bets as to which slave could drink the most whiskey and in "this way succeed in getting whole multitudes to drink to excess."* ***Note:*** *Both of these quotes reinforce the same idea, so the analysis goes after the second quote.*
Analyze the quote	**Example**
This is where you explain how this quote is evidence of Douglass's position	*If slavery civilized slaves, then slaveholders would not intentionally try to make slaves drink too much. This example illustrates that slaveholders, in fact, encouraged slaves to be uncivilized, and immoral.*

Quote Sandwich in Action

Name: ____

Date: ____

Text of Essay	Analyzing Structure
Defenders of slavery often argued that slavery supported a natural order in society, but Douglass argues that slavery disrupts the natural order because it destroys family relationships. He describes the dynamics of his own family, which were distorted by slavery. Douglass's father was, in fact, his white master. He goes on to explain that this was very common, and this created a situation in which a father, instead of caring for his child, would "sell his own children to human flesh-mongers" (Chapter 1). If they did not, the father would be compelled to "stand by and see one white son tie up his brother . . . and ply the gory lash to his naked back" (Chapter 1). Many Northerners believed fathers should care for their children and brothers should stand together, and the images of a father selling his own children and a brother whipping his brother horrified them. These examples help to convey Douglass's position that slavery destroys natural family relationships.	In this paragraph, notice the following elements: 1. Position of people who defend slavery 2. Douglass's position 3. Evidence of Douglass's position—sandwiched with context 4. **Analysis**: How this evidence conveys Douglass's position. How it disproves the position of people who supported slavery. 5. Concluding sentence
Another common misconception held by Northerners who defended slavery was that slavery civilized the African people. In order to counter this belief, Douglass uses the annual holidays slaves got from their slaveholders as an example. Every year between Christmas and New Year's, slaves were allowed to have time off. However, slaveholders, instead of encouraging a slave to participate in uplifting activities, would "adopt various plans to make him drunk" (Chapter 10). One such plan was taking bets as to which slave could drink the most whiskey and in "this way succeed in getting whole multitudes to drink to excess" (Chapter 10). If slavery civilized slaves, then slaveholders would not intentionally try to make slaves drink too much. This example illustrates that slaveholders, in fact, encouraged slaves to be uncivilized and immoral.	After you read this paragraph, answer the following question: 6. What is missing from this paragraph? What suggestions would you have for the author of this body paragraph?

Grades 6–8 Expository Writing Evaluation Rubric

Source: Based on a rubric created for the New York State Common Core Curriculum.

SCORE	A (90–100)	B (80–89)	C (70–79)	D (65–69)	F (< 65)
CRITERIA	Exceeds Expectations	Meets Expectations	Below Expectations	Needs Improvement	Unacceptable
CONTENT AND ANALYSIS: the extent to which the essay conveys complex ideas and information clearly and accurately in order to support claims in an analysis of topics or texts	Clearly introduce a topic in a manner that is compelling and follows logically from the task and purpose (deep understanding) Demonstrate insightful (a deeper meaning) analysis of the text(s)	Clearly introduce a topic in a manner that follows from the task and purpose Demonstrate grade-appropriate analysis of the text(s)	Introduce a topic in a manner that follows generally from the task and purpose Demonstrate only a factual comprehension of the text(s)	Introduce a topic in a manner that does not logically follow from the task and purpose Demonstrate little understanding of the text(s)	Demonstrate a lack of comprehension of the text(s) or task
COMMAND OF EVIDENCE: the extent to which the essay presents evidence from the provided texts to support analysis and reflection	Develop the topic with relevant, well-chosen facts, definitions, concrete details, quotations, or other information and examples from the text(s) Sustain (continue) use of varied, relevant evidence	Develop the topic with relevant facts, definitions, details, quotations, or other information and examples from the text(s) Sustain (continue) the use of relevant evidence, with some lack of variety	Partially develop the topic of the essay with the use of some textual evidence, some of which may be irrelevant Use relevant evidence sometimes (inconsistently)	Demonstrate an attempt to use evidence, but only develop ideas with minimal, occasional evidence that is generally invalid or irrelevant (off topic/inaccurate)	Provide no evidence or provide evidence that is completely irrelevant (off-topic)

COHERENCE, ORGANIZATION, AND STYLE: the extent to which the essay logically organizes complex ideas, concepts, and information using formal style and precise language	Exhibit clear organization, with the skillful use of appropriate and varied transitions to create a unified whole and enhance meaning Establish and maintain a formal style, using grade-appropriate, stylistically sophisticated language and subject/ text-specific vocabulary that are easy to read Provide a concluding statement or section that is compelling and follows clearly from the topic	Exhibit clear organization, with the use of appropriate transitions to create a flow of ideas Establish and maintain a formal style using precise language and subject/text-specific vocabulary Provide a concluding statement or section that follows from the topic and information presented	Exhibit some attempt at organization, with inconsistent use of transitions (sometimes) Establish but fail to maintain (did not keep up) a formal style, with inconsistent use of language and subject/text-specific vocabulary Provide a concluding statement or section that follows generally from the topic and information presented	Exhibit little attempt at organization, or attempts to organize are irrelevant to the task Lack a formal style, using language that is imprecise or inappropriate for the text(s) and task Provide a concluding statement or section that is illogical or unrelated to the topic and information presented	Exhibit no evidence of organization Use language that is predominantly incoherent or copied directly from the text(s) Do not provide a concluding statement or section
CONTROL OF CONVENTIONS: the extent to which the essay demonstrates command of the conventions of standard English grammar, usage, capitalization, punctuation, and spelling	Demonstrate command of conventions, with few errors	Demonstrate command of conventions, with occasional errors that do not hinder comprehension	Demonstrate beginning command of conventions, with some errors that may hinder comprehension (make it hard to read)	Demonstrate a lack of command of conventions, with frequent errors that hinder comprehension (make it hard to read)	Are minimal, making grading of conventions unreliable

End-of-Unit Assessment

Analyzing Douglass's Purpose in *Narrative of the Life of Frederick Douglass*

Name: ______________________________

Date: ______________________________

Directions: In a well-reasoned and coherent essay, please answer the following prompt:

In his *Narrative,* Frederick Douglass explains his purpose is to throw "light on the American slave system." Which aspects of slavery does his narrative bring to light? How does his position differ from that of those who defended slavery? How does he use his story to support his position?

Your essay should demonstrate your progress toward the following learning targets:

- I can write an organized essay that explains the position of Frederick Douglass with relevant and well-chosen examples.
- In my essay, I can analyze how Frederick Douglass distinguished his positions from those of his audience.
- In my essay, I can use evidence effectively.

Entry Task

Introducing the Children's Book

Name: ____________________

Date: ____________________

Directions: Complete this task individually. Read the prompt and underline five important verbs that clarify what you will do for these assessments. Then complete the sentence stems at the bottom of the page.

End-of-Unit Assessment and Performance Task Prompt

Choose one episode from *Narrative of the Life of Frederick Douglass.* Write and plan the illustrations for a children's book that tells this story in a way that is appropriate to your audience, conveys a message that is broadly applicable to situations beyond the story, and uses language to create a powerful story. Your story should demonstrate your knowledge of the life of Frederick Douglass and of narrative techniques.

Then, revise your text and illustrate your children's book. Your **final, publishable version** will be assessed using the Module 3 Performance Task Rubric.

Learning Targets (from W.7.3, W.7.5)

- I can write a narrative text about an event from *Narrative of the Life of Frederick Douglass* using relevant details and event sequences that make sense.
- I can use effective narrative techniques to develop the character and events in the narrative.
- I can provide a conclusion that reflects on the narrated experience of Frederick Douglass and connects it to a larger, more universal message.
- With support from peers and adults, I can use a writing process to ensure that purpose and audience have been addressed.

Audience	Upper elementary school
Purpose	To retell one of the events from the life of Fredrick Douglass in an engaging and creative way

To connect Frederick Douglass's experience to a universal human truth.

Book length	6–8 pages (300–500 words)
Illustrations	4 (including cover)
Timing	You will have limited class time for planning, peer review, writing, and illustrating. You will complete a portion of the work at home.

Your **Children's Book Storyboards** with a polished version of your text and a rough sketch of your illustrations are your End-of-Unit Assessment and are due on ______________________.

In order to be successful on this project, I need . . .

____

____

____

A potential problem I see is . . .

____

____

____

How a Narrative Is Different from a Summary Reference Sheet

Example from *The Last Day of Slavery*	A Narrative . . .		A Summary . . .
"He hid in the woods and ate wild berries, drank water from a shallow stream." (page 17)	Develops setting with sensory descriptive detail	Establishes **context**	Names setting
"In front of the fire, he cleaned Frederick's wounds, gave him Indian corn to eat." (page 19)	Develops character with "show-not-tell" description—using some adjectives but also nouns, strong verbs, and dialogue		Names characters and describes them with adjectives and verbs
"He knew that Frederick had to be broken soon . . . Even when he sat down to eat his lunch, Covey watched him with a cold eye." (page 13)	Describes events that illustrate the conflict, but usually does not explicitly name it	Establishes **conflict**	Names the conflict
There are many examples. Here is one: "While they kicked and hit each other, while they wrestled in the dirt, the slaves watched in disbelief." (page 23)	"Shows" the most important events unfolding by using sensory description, strong verbs, and dialogue		

Example from *The Last Day of Slavery*	A Narrative . . .		A Summary . . .
There are many examples. Here is one: "While they kicked and hit each other, while they wrestled in the dirt, the slaves watched in disbelief." (page 23)	"Shows" the most important events unfolding by using sensory description, strong verbs, and dialogue	**Climbing** steps: Tells the story in logical sequence Has a clear climax	Names the important points of action Uses some description and strong verbs
"When Frederick was seventeen . . ." (page 13) "One day . . ." (page 15) "That night . . ." (page 17)	Uses transitional words such as *then, next,* and so on		Uses transitional words such as *then, next,* and so on
"Lying in the dark of the woods, he wished he were an animal himself: a creature with fur and claws to protect himself." (page 17)	Focuses on thoughts and emotions of the character		Mentions thoughts and emotions of characters in passing
"When the fight was over, the breaker looked at Frederick with new eyes. Fear was in his eyes, but also respect." (page 26) "He told himself that he would never think or act like a slave again." (page 27)	Shows the resolution of the conflict Shows character growth Implies a theme or universal truth but usually does not explicitly say it	Provides a **conclusion**	Sums up the events of the story Names the resolution of the conflict Directly states character growth and change

EXPEDITIONARY
LEARNING

Narrative Writer's Toolbox Anchor Chart

Tool	Possible Function

EXPEDITIONARY
LEARNING

Sentence Practice Worksheet

Directions: Read the following phrases. Pick the sentence that most correctly combines the phrases.

1. which was delicious

   The burrito

   was full of black beans

   a. The burrito, which was delicious, was full of black beans.

   b. The burrito was full of black beans which was delicious.

2. The burrito

   which were spilling out of it

   was full of black beans

   a. The burrito, which were spilling out of it, was full of black beans.

   b. The burrito was full of black beans, which were spilling out of it.

3. the black beans

   which were spilling out of the burrito

   were spicy and delicious

   a. The black beans, which were spilling out of the burrito, were spicy and delicious.

   b. The black beans were spicy and delicious, which were spilling out of the burrito.

4. I ate

   a burrito

   one day for lunch

   chips and salsa

   that was full of black beans and cheese

   a. One day for lunch, I ate a burrito that was full of black beans and cheese and chips and salsa.

   b. One day for lunch, I ate chips and salsa and a burrito that was full of black beans and cheese.

Now you try. Combine the dependent and independent clauses into grammatically correct sentences. Then combine them into a grammatically incorrect sentence and be prepared to explain why it is incorrect.

5. the ant

   marched along the ground

   which was carrying a huge leaf

   a. Correct sentence:

   ____

   b. Incorrect sentence:

   ____

6. as he marched along the ground

   the ant

   stumbled a little

   which was carrying a huge leaf

   a. Correct sentence:

   ____

   b. Incorrect sentence: I wouldn't march along the ground to ring

7. the ant

   who was spinning a web

   which was marching along the ground

   stumbled in front of a spider

   a. Correct sentence:

   ____

   b. Incorrect sentence: Be cause I ta Dee's n't go that way

8. the ant

   the spider

   which was carrying a large leaf

   was attacked by

   who was desperately hungry

   a. Correct sentence: The spider was attack by the ant which was carring a large leaf who was depperately hungry

   b. Incorrect sentence:

9. and won

   an ant

   fought a spider

   one summer day

   which was full of unusual events

   who was carrying a huge leaf at the time

   a. Correct sentence:

   b. Incorrect sentence:

Entry Task

Summing It Up

Name: ______________________________

Date: ______________________________

Part I

Directions: Complete this task individually.

These are the last lines of *Frederick Douglass: The Last Day of Slavery*:

> "That night, while he lay by the fire, Frederick thought about his mother. He remembered how she had walked all night, across the frozen fields, just to hold him.
>
> He told himself that he would never think or act like a slave again. He promised his mother that one day he would escape, that all slaves would be free.
>
> Frederick looked up into the sky and saw the moon drifting through the clouds.
>
> After the moon came a star, pale and far off, but burning in the sky."

1. What is the theme that Frederick reflects on in these last few lines?

   ____

2. The star that he sees "pale and far off but burning" is symbolic to him. What does the star represent to Frederick?

   ____

Part II

Directions: With a partner, articulate a thematic statement for two of the episodes we read as a class.

Episode	Episode
That night, while he lay by the fire, Frederick thought . . .	That night, while he lay by the fire, Frederick thought . . .
He told himself that . . .	He told himself that . . .

EXPEDITIONARY LEARNING

Children's Book Scavenger Hunt

Name: ____________________

Date: ____________________

I. Scavenger Hunt

Directions: Read the children's book provided and answer the questions in the first column. Then look for the author's use of narrative techniques. When you find evidence of one, note it in the third column.

Book Title:

Elements of a Story	Can You Find . . .	Example from Text (with page number)
What is the setting?	. . . one **sensory detail** that helped you imagine the setting?	
Who is the main character?	. . . when the author **shows** you a character trait instead of just telling you?	
What is the central conflict?	. . . where the author **shows** you the conflict instead of telling you?	
What happens in the story?	. . . a **strong verb**? . . . an example of **dialogue**? . . . three **vivid words** or **precise adjectives**?	
Does the author show what the characters think or feel?	. . . one thought-shot?	
What is the resolution?	. . . some concluding sentences that lead the reader to the thematic statement that the story is implying?	

II. Zooming In

Directions: Think for a moment about where the author zoomed in on the action or characters and where the author did not.

1. Describe one event the author zoomed in on. Why is this event important enough to zoom in on? What tools did the author use to magnify this event?

   ____

   ____

   ____

2. Describe a place that the author paused to give the reader a thought-shot. Why was it important for us to know the thoughts of the character at this time?

   ____

   ____

   ____

3. Describe one event the author moved quickly over. Why is this event not important enough to zoom in on?

   ____

   ____

   ____

III. Looking at Pictures

Directions: Now spend a few minutes looking at the pictures. Pick one illustration to focus on. What do you notice? Why? What part of the text did this author choose to illustrate? Make some notes for yourself here. Be prepared to share out with a partner.

____

____

____

IV. Tell a Friend

(You'll do this in the next lesson.)

Directions: Now share what you found with your small group. Start with these sentence stems:

My story was powerful/was not powerful because . . .

____

____

____

I noticed that the author of this book . . .

____

____

____

As you discuss, use this as an opportunity to practice using these sentence stems that can help you on your Mid-Unit Assessment.

Questions to encourage discussion:

Why did you think . . . ?

Did you consider . . . ?

Could you explain your thinking about . . . ?

I hear you saying . . . Is that right?

Respectful responses that encourage discussion:

I'm glad you said . . .

I hadn't thought of . . .

I see it differently because . . .

I hear you saying . . . and now I think . . .

Putting Sentences Together

Name: ______________________________

Date: ______________________________

Directions: Using the collections of phrases and sentences below, make at least three grammatically correct sentences. You can add words, rearrange existing words, or change verbs tense if you need to.

Model	Dog, getting on my nerves, barking

The dog, which was barking, was getting on my nerves.

The barking dog was getting on my nerves.

The dog, which was getting on my nerves, wouldn't stop barking.

Because he was barking, the dog was getting on my nerves.

Combining phrases	Day, sunny, was starting to get cloudy
	There was someone He looked down the hall didn't recognize
Combining sentences	Frederick learned to read. Reading opened up a whole new world to him. Frederick got a taste of freedom.
	Frederick devised a daring plan. It was a plan full of danger. The plan filled him with hope.

Entry Task

Preparing for the Mid-Unit Assessment, Part 1

Name: ______________________________

Date: ______________________________

Directions: Please complete this task individually. Read over the assessment prompt and criteria. Then answer the questions.

Mid-Unit Assessment Prompt

Tomorrow you will participate in a Writer's Roundtable. You will present your Children's Book Plan to the group and talk about the questions and concerns you have. This is an excellent chance for you to get feedback on your Children's Book Plan so far. You also help your fellow classmates by critiquing their plans thoughtfully. In addition, this activity demonstrates how well you can reach the following learning targets:

- I can effectively engage in discussions with diverse partners about seventh-grade topics, texts, and issues.
- I can follow rules for collegial discussions and track my progress toward a specific goal.
- I can pose questions that elicit elaboration and respond to the questions and comments of others with relevant observations.
- I can acknowledge new information expressed by others and, when warranted, modify my own views.

Speaking and Listening Criteria

What it will look like when I reach the learning targets:	Sentence stems that may help me:
___ Asks relevant, helpful questions that elicit elaboration	Why did you think . . . ? Did you consider . . . ?
___ Seeks to clarify and understand other perspectives, especially when they differ from one's own	Could you explain your thinking about . . . ? I hear you saying . . . Is that right? Do you agree that . . . ?

___ Makes helpful observations about another's work	I hear you saying . . . I see you have . . . A real strength of this part is . . . This part needs a little work because . . .
___ Seeks out and respectfully acknowledges others' ideas	I'd like to hear your thoughts on . . . I'm glad you said . . . I hadn't thought of . . . I see it differently because . . .
___ Does not dominate conversation	I'd like to hear your thoughts on . . .

1. What do you need to do to be successful in the group discussion tomorrow?

____

____

____

2. What are some potential pitfalls? How will you avoid them?

____

____

____

Ladder to Success Anchor Chart

Children's Book
Final Version—Publishable!
Performance Task

Teacher Feedback	I Heart Revision Check-in	Begin Final Illustrations

Children's Book Storyboards
Second Draft
End-of-Unit Assessment

Self-Assessment with the Rubric		I Heart Revision Check-in

Children's Book Storyboards
Second Half—First Draft

Peer Edit		I Heart Revision Check-in

Children's Book Storyboards
First Half—First Draft

Writer's Roundtable Mid-Unit Assessment Part 1		I Heart Revision Check-in

My Children's Book Plan

Analysis Note-Catcher

My Children's Book Plan

Name: ____

Date: ____

Directions: Now you will plan your children's story. When you begin writing, use this plan as a guide. You will probably make small adjustments as you write. As you plan, think carefully about where you will zoom in and be more detailed; do it deliberately and only in moments of the story that need to be examined closely. You may have six to eight pages in your book. You must have at least five pages planned for the Writer's Roundtable tomorrow.

Gist of the Story

____

Thematic Statement

____

____

Page Number	**Gist of the Text** *** Narrative tool I will use**	**Gist of Illustration** (*Remember:* Not every page needs an illustration. Choose the pages that best lend themselves to images.)	**Step on the Narrative Arc**
Model	*Douglass was born on a plantation. He didn't know his mother.* ** Sensory details: slept with "miserable blankets" on a "cold, damp floor"* ** Showing character traits: mother walking all night*	*FD as a baby with a shadowy, blurry image of his mother standing over him*	*Establishing context—setting, character, and central conflict*
1			

2			
3			
4			
5			
6			
7			

My Takeaway from the Writer's Roundtable:

(Note: Do this during discussion tomorrow)

Exit Ticket

Planning for the Mid-Unit Assessment, Part 1

Name: ____________________

Date: ____________________

How confident are you in your Children's Book Plan? Why?

____

____

____

____

What are you still unclear about? How could talking it over with your peers help address your concerns?

____

____

____

____

What five questions will you ask your group tomorrow? Here are some examples to get you started (you may use these example questions—they're useful!):

- I'm thinking of zooming in on these moments. Do they seem critical to the story?
- What pages should have an illustration?
- Is my thematic statement appropriate to the story?

1. ____________________
   ____
2. ____________________
   ____
3. ____________________
   ____
4. ____________________
   ____
5. ____________________
   ____

EXPEDITIONARY
LEARNING

Sentence Practice Homework

Name: ______________________________

Date: ______________________________

Directions: Use this practice sheet to help you prepare for the Mid-Unit Assessment, Part 2.

Reading Complex Sentences

1. When we got halfway to St. Michael's, while the constables in charge were looking ahead, Henry inquired of me what he should do with his pass.

   Underline the main clause of the sentence.

2. We were spreading manure; and all at once, while thus engaged, I was overwhelmed with an indescribable feeling, in the fullness of which I turned to Sandy, who was nearby, and said, "We are betrayed!"

   Underline the main clause of the sentence.

   Which noun does the phrase "who was nearby" modify?

3. During the scuffle, I managed—I know not how—to get my pass out and, without being discovered, put it into the fire.

   Underline the main clause of the sentence.

   The phrase "without being discovered" modifies which phrase: "put it into the fire" or "I know not how"?

Writing Complex Sentences

1. Combine these three phrases into a grammatically correct sentence:

   Frederick Douglass was a runaway slave

   who wrote an autobiography

   Frederick Douglass was a passionate abolitionist

   ____

   ____

   ____

   ____

2. Combine these phrases into a grammatically correct sentence:

   Mrs. Auld surprised Frederick by looking at him kindly

   who had never owned slaves before

3. Combine these three sentences into a grammatically correct sentence:

   A slave who tried to run away faced many dangers.

   Some of the dangers a slave faced were crossing treacherous terrain, being chased by bloodthirsty dogs, and starving to death.

   Many slaves didn't dare to run away.

Correct the following sentences. (*Note:* There is more than one correct answer.)

1. Frederick saw slaves being beaten, this changed his life and made him wonder how human beings could treat each other this way.

2. When he escaped to the North, Frederick was amazed at the people and the kindness they offered, who were so hard working.

3. Frederick was dizzy and hot but he knew if he didn't get up.

4. Because many slaves were terrified of being caught.

5. When a slave sings, it is not because he is happy and carefree. But because he has no other way to express his deep sadness.

EXPEDITIONARY
LEARNING

Writer's Roundtable

Peer Observation

Name: ______________________________

Date: ______________________________

Student Name and Date: Notes/Comments:	**Criteria** ___ Asks relevant, helpful questions that elicit elaboration ___ Makes thoughtful observations about another's work ___ Seeks out and respectfully acknowledges others' ideas ___ Seeks to clarify other perspectives, especially when they differ from one's own ___ Does not dominate conversation

Student Name and Date: Notes/Comments:	**Criteria** ___ Asks relevant, helpful questions that elicit elaboration ___ Makes thoughtful observations about another's work ___ Seeks out and respectfully acknowledges others' ideas ___ Seeks to clarify other perspectives, especially when they differ from one's own ___ Does not dominate conversation

Student Name and Date: Notes/Comments:	**Criteria** ___ Asks relevant, helpful questions that elicit elaboration ___ Makes thoughtful observations about another's work ___ Seeks out and respectfully acknowledges others' ideas ___ Seeks to clarify other perspectives, especially when they differ from one's own ___ Does not dominate conversation

Student Name and Date: Notes/Comments:	**Criteria** ____ Asks relevant, helpful questions that elicit elaboration ____ Makes thoughtful observations about another's work ____ Seeks out and respectfully acknowledges others' ideas ____ Seeks to clarify other perspectives, especially when they differ from one's own ____ Does not dominate conversation

Student Name and Date: Notes/Comments:	**Criteria** ____ Asks relevant, helpful questions that elicit elaboration ____ Makes thoughtful observations about another's work ____ Seeks out and respectfully acknowledges others' ideas ____ Seeks to clarify other perspectives, especially when they differ from one's own ____ Does not dominate conversation

Student Name and Date: Notes/Comments:	**Criteria** ____ Asks relevant, helpful questions that elicit elaboration ____ Makes thoughtful observations about another's work ____ Seeks out and respectfully acknowledges others' ideas ____ Seeks to clarify other perspectives, especially when they differ from one's own ____ Does not dominate conversation

EXPEDITIONARY LEARNING

Mid-Unit Assessment, Part 1

Writer's Roundtable

Self-Assessment

Name: ______________________________

Date: ______________________________

Directions: As you participate in the Writer's Roundtable today, please track the kinds of comments and questions you are asking. For each comment, put a checkmark next to each criterion you are addressing. A good way to gauge if you are dominating the conversation is whether you have many checkmarks for each criterion. If you notice this happening, invite others into the conversation.

Speaking and Listening Criteria

Criteria	Sentence stems that may help me:
___ Asks relevant, helpful questions that elicit elaboration	Why did you think . . . ? Did you consider . . . ?
___ Seeks to clarify and understand other perspectives, especially when they differ from one's own	Could you explain your thinking about . . . ? I hear you saying . . . Is that right? Do you agree that . . . ?
___ Makes helpful observations about another's work	I hear you saying . . . I see you have . . . A real strength of this part is . . . This part needs a little work because . . .
___ Seeks out and respectfully acknowledges others' ideas	I'd like to hear your thoughts on . . . I'm glad you said . . . I hadn't thought of . . . I see it differently because . . .
___ Does not dominate conversation	I'd like to hear your thoughts on . . .

Based on the criteria above, write a short paragraph that evaluates your performance in the Writer's Roundtable. Consider these questions: What were your strengths? What was the best question you asked? Why? What were your struggles?

EXPEDITIONARY LEARNING

Entry Task

I Heart Revisions

Name: ______________________________

Date: ______________________________

Directions: A vital part of the writing process is feedback and revision. You will have several opportunities to revise your children's book. This chart helps you track your feedback and subsequent plans for revision. It also helps you demonstrate how well you have reached the following learning target:

- With support from peers and adults, I can use a writing process to ensure that purpose and audience have been addressed.

Revision Point 1: Writer's Roundtable

Comments		My Reaction
Strengths:	Suggestions for revision:	I agree/disagree with this suggestion because . . . Based on these comments, I will . . . because . . .

Revision Point 2: Partner Read

Comments		My Reaction
Strengths:	Suggestions for revision:	I agree/disagree with this suggestion because . . . Based on these comments, I will . . . because . . .

Revision Point 3: Myself **Date** ___________

Comments		My Reaction
Strengths:	Suggestions for revision:	I agree/disagree with this suggestion because . . . Based on these comments, I will . . . because . . .

Revision Point 4: Teacher Feedback

Comments		My Reaction
Strengths:	Suggestions for revision:	I agree/disagree with this suggestion because . . . Based on these comments, I will . . . because . . .

Mid-Unit Assessment, Part 2

Sentence Structure Quiz

Name: ____

Date: ____

Part I. Reading Complex Sentences

Directions: Read the following sentences and answer the questions that follow.

1. Colonel Lloyd kept a large and finely cultivated garden, which afforded almost constant employment for four men, besides the chief gardener, Mr. M'Durmond.
   a. Underline the main clause of the sentence.
   b. What does the phrase that begins "which afforded almost constant employment for four men" modify?

   ____

2. Its excellent fruit was quite a temptation to the hungry swarms of boys, as well as to older slaves, few of whom had the virtue or the vice to resist it.
   a. Underline the main clause of the sentence.
   b. What two nouns does the phrase that begins "few of whom" modify?

   ____

Part II: Writing Complex Sentences

1. Combine the two sentences below into one sentence. You may change words but not meaning.

   I have had two masters.

   My first master was called Captain Anthony.

   ____

   ____

   ____

2. Combine the ideas below into one sentence. You may rearrange the order of the phrases and change words but not meaning.

   One morning in September

   Anthony was in ninth grade

   He slept late

   He missed the bus

Part III: Correcting Sentences

Directions: Make the sentences below into correctly written complete sentences. You may add or change words and punctuation.

1. The slaves on the plantation are hardworking. And get little sleep.

2. The slaveholders and their families often have everything taken care of for them by their slaves, they enjoy an easier lifestyle.

3. Slaves are treated poorly, they are always blamed for things that are not really their fault, they suffer from lack of food and clothing.

4. One slave Frederick Douglass.

5. Frederick Douglass's mother died when he was seven, who lived on a different plantation.

EXPEDITIONARY LEARNING

Sharpening Your Tools, Part 1

Show-Not-Tell and Sensory Details

From *Frederick Douglass: The Last Day of Slavery*

Frederick Douglass was born a slave.

He never knew his father and saw his mother only a few times. She walked all night through freezing woods, across fields burned white by the moon.

She walked all night just to hold him.

Frederick remembered her face for the rest of his life: dark skin and warm eyes, a mouth that broke into a loving smile.

1. What sensory details establish setting?

____

____

____

2. What character does the author zoom in on? Why is that character important?

____

____

____

3. Mr. Miller, the author, could have told us that Frederick's mother was kind. Instead he *showed* she was kind (an adjective) by using nouns and verbs. What verb shows she is kind? What nouns?

____

____

____

Tell (uses bland adjectives)	Show (use nouns and verbs and vivid adjectives)
Mrs. Auld was a kind person.	
Frederick was scared.	
Covey was mean.	

EXPEDITIONARY LEARNING

Children's Book Storyboard

Name: ______________________________

Date: ______________________________

First Draft of Text

____

____

____

____

____

____

____

____

____

____

Second Draft of Text

____

____

____

____

____

____

____

____

____

____

Directions: Plan what each page of your story will look like. The illustration can be a rough sketch. The text should be carefully planned, revised, and finalized before you turn it in for the End-of-Unit Assessment.

Page Number: ______

Teacher Feedback: ________________________________

Illustration (if applicable)

EXPEDITIONARY
LEARNING

Sharpening Your Tools, Part 2

Entry Task

Name: ______________________________

Date: ______________________________

Directions: Read the following paragraphs. They both narrate the same event from *The Last Day of Slavery*.

Version 1

One day, Frederick was working in the tobacco barn. It was a hot day, and he soon grew tired. Dizzy and sick, he stumbled into the light and fell down beneath an oak tree. The breaker told Frederick to get up and finish his work. Frederick tried to explain, but Covey wouldn't listen.

Frederick felt the blow of the hickory stick against his head. The breaker hit him again and again, until he crawled into the barn.

Version 2

One day, Frederick was in the barn. He got really sick. Covey got mad and yelled at him. Frederick couldn't get up so Covey hit him a lot. Frederick got away.

1. Which version do you think is more clear and vivid, and better helps the reader understand what is happening? Why?

   ____

   ____

   ____

2. Which narrative tools do you see the author using in these paragraphs?

   ____

   ____

   ____

Sharpening Your Tools: Side-by-Side Comparison

Version 1	Version 2	
One day, Frederick was working in the tobacco barn.	One day, Frederick was in the barn.	Precise description: tobacco Strong action verb: working
It was a hot day, and he soon grew tired. Dizzy and sick, he stumbled into the light and fell down beneath an oak tree.	He got really sick.	Sensory word: hot Precise description: dizzy, oak tree Strong verb: stumbled
The breaker told Frederick to get up and finish his work.	Covey got mad and yelled at him.	Precise description: breaker Strong verb: get up and finish
Frederick tried to explain, but Covey wouldn't listen. Frederick felt the blow of the hickory stick against his head.	Frederick couldn't get up so Covey hit him a lot.	Strong verb: wouldn't listen Strong verb: felt the blow Precise description: hickory stick
The breaker hit him again and again, until he crawled into the barn.	Frederick got away.	Strong verb: crawled

A Short List of Strong Verbs

General verbs	Vivid verbs
work	toil, labor, struggle, strain
like	admire, adore, appreciate, cherish, be fond of, worship
dislike	abhor, abominate, avoid, condemn, deplore, despise, detest, disapprove, hate, loathe, resent, scorn, shun
hit	beat, knock, box, bump, slap, whack, bang
run	dart, dash, jog, lope, scamper, scurry, sprint
said	whispered, sputtered, squeaked, stammered, demanded, begged, interrupted, insisted, murmured, uttered, mumbled, cried, roared, proposed
walk	amble, hike, march, plod, saunter, stroll, stride, trek, trudge
want	wish, crave, long for, yearn, hunger

EXPEDITIONARY
LEARNING

Peer Editing Checklist

First Draft

Author's Name: ____________________

Editor's Name: ____________________

Directions: Read your partner's page carefully. Then fill out the checklist below. Not every page will have all the items on the list. Write your specific feedback in the space below.

Page _____

_____ Uses powerful language that is precise, relevant, and descriptive

_____ The text "shows" the action rather than "tells" by using:

- ___ Sensory description
- ___ Strong verbs
- ___ Precise, vivid word choice
- ___ Dialogue

_____ Language is appropriate for audience

_____ Uses a variety of sentence types

_____ Follows narrative arc

_____ Page 1 or 2: Establishes context (setting, characters, and conflict)

_____ Pages 2–5: Uses transitional words to explain the logical sequence of events

_____ Last page: Provides a thought-provoking and relevant reflection on a universal truth

Praise	Questions	Suggestions

Page _____

_____ Uses powerful language that is precise, relevant, and descriptive

_____ The text "shows" the action rather than "tells" by using:

- ___ Sensory description
- ___ Strong verbs
- ___ Precise, vivid word choice
- ___ Dialogue

_____ Language is appropriate for audience

_____ Uses a variety of sentence types

_____ Follows narrative arc

_____ Page 1 or 2: Establishes context (setting, characters, and conflict)

_____ Pages 2–5: Uses transitional words to explain the logical sequence of events

_____ Last page: Provides a thought-provoking and relevant reflection on a universal truth

Praise	Questions	Suggestions

Independent Reading Check-In

Name: ______________________________

Date: ______________________________

Directions: Complete this task individually. Look back through the pages you've recently read and pick a short passage (three or four sentences) where you can see the narrative tools at work. Copy the passage into the left-hand column. Then write a blander, less engaging version of the text that has no narrative tools in the right-hand column.

Original Passage	Less Vivid Version

1. Explain why you picked this passage. What narrative technique do you see?

____

____

____

2. Why did the author zoom in here? Explain the overall significance of this character or event.

____

____

____

Sharpening Your Tools, Part 3

Dialogue and Figurative Language

Version 1

"What are you doing?!" demanded Mr. Auld as he walked in on Mrs. Auld teaching Frederick his ABCs.

"I'm teaching little Freddy here his ABCs. Did you know this poor young man doesn't even know his ABCs? Imagine such a thing!"

"No, YOU imagine! Wife, do you know what would happen if you teach this slave to read? Why . . . he'll get ideas! Dangerous ideas! He would be unfit to be a slave. He'll be unhappy with his God-given role. Do you want that? Wife, you have forgotten that this is not a young man, this is a slave! Now stop this at once!"

Mrs. Auld's eyes filled with tears. "I was just trying to help!" she cried as she fled from the room.

That changed everything. It was if a light had been switched off in Mrs. Auld's heart. She grew suspicious of Frederick, and instead of looking for ways to be kind to him, she tried to catch him being disobedient. If she saw him looking at a newspaper, she would snatch it away, slap his hand, and begin shrieking about the ingratitude of slaves. Frederick missed his kind mistress.

Version 2

However, the experience of owning a slave soon corrupted her. One day her husband came home and saw her trying to teach Frederick his letters. Her husband forbade her from teaching Frederick to read, saying that it spoiled a slave to learn to read. She then turned into a "demon" and began to watch his every move. When she caught him holding a newspaper, she would snatch it away and yell at him.

Version 3

"What are you doing?!" demanded Mr. Auld as he walked in on Mrs. Auld teaching Frederick his ABCs.

"What do you mean?" Mrs. Auld asked innocently.

"I mean, what are you doing right now?" Mr. Auld insisted. Frederick looked around nervously like a cat stuck in a tree.

"I'm teaching little Freddy here his ABCs. Did you know this poor young man doesn't even know his ABCs? Imagine such a thing!"

"You're teaching him what?" Mr. Auld was so angry he could barely speak. It was as if his tongue were tied.

"His ABCs."

"His ABCs! Why . . . why . . ." Mr. Auld sputtered out like an old car engine.

"I mean to have no learning, imagine!" Mrs. Auld continued, oblivious to her husband's feelings.

"No, YOU imagine! Wife, do you know what would happen if you teach this slave to read? Why . . . he'll get ideas! Dangerous ideas! He would be unfit to be a slave. He'll be unhappy with his God-given role. Do you want that? Wife, you have forgotten that this is not a young man, this is a slave! Now stop this at once!"

"What? What do you mean?"

"You know what I mean! Are you an idiot? You can't teach a slave to read. I can't say it any clearer!"

Mrs. Auld's eyes filled with tears like a waterfall. "I was just trying to help!" she cried as she fled from the room.

EXPEDITIONARY
LEARNING

Entry Task

Looking at the Rubric

Name: ______________________________

Date: ______________________________

Directions: Complete this task individually. Read through each column. Underline the two most important words in each box.

Children's Book Based on Frederick Douglass Rubric (Module 7.3 Performance Task)

	3	2	1
Content	The author demonstrates an understanding of the characters and events in the *Narrative of the Life of Frederick Douglass.* The story is appropriate for children.	The author demonstrates a limited understanding of the characters and events in the *Narrative.* The story is somewhat appropriate for children.	The author demonstrates little understanding of the characters and events in the *Narrative.* The story does not seem particularly suited to any specific audience.
Techniques	The author uses narrative tools (such as strong verbs, show-not-tell details, precise word choice, dialogue, and so on) thoughtfully and deliberately to make an engaging story where the meaning is clear to the reader. The story follows the narrative arc, including establishing setting, following a logical sequence of events, and providing a conclusion. The story concludes with a thoughtful and engaging thematic statement.	The author uses the narrative tools somewhat appropriately but inconsistently. The story follows the narrative arc. The story concludes with a thematic statement.	The author uses very few narrative tools or uses them indiscriminately, without a clear connection to the story. The story does not include all the steps on the narrative arc. The story concludes with a confusing thematic statement or the thematic statement is missing.

Conventions	The story follows the written conventions appropriate for seventh grade with special attention to sentence structure, spelling, and comma use.	The story follows the written conventions appropriate for seventh grade inconsistently, especially in these areas: sentence structure, spelling, and comma use.	The story does not follow the written conventions appropriate for seventh grade, especially in these areas: sentence structure, spelling, and comma use.
Revisions	The author used feedback from others and the writing process to make meaningful revisions.	The author used feedback from others and the writing process to make limited revisions.	The author did not use feedback from others or the writing process to make meaningful revisions.

Entry Task

Using Commas with Adjectives

Name: ____________________

Date: ____________________

Directions: Punctuate these sentences correctly.

1. The sweet frosty milkshake was delicious.

   ____

2. The noise of the freeway was loud relentless and depressing.

   ____

3. I knew the electricity was out because the school hall was dark cold and deserted.

   ____

4. The shiny electric car was driving down the winding curvy road.

   ____

5. I pulled on a thick cotton sweater and went outside into the crisp fall day.

   ____

6. The cheerful store clerk described the sales to me in a voice that was enthusiastic melodic and frankly a little creepy.

   ____

EXPEDITIONARY
LEARNING

Using Commas with Adjectives Answer Key

Directions: Use this answer key to check your work.

1. The sweet, frosty milkshake was delicious.

2. The noise of the freeway was loud, relentless, and depressing.

3. I knew the electricity was out because the school hall was dark, cold, and deserted.

4. The shiny electric car was driving down the winding, curvy road.

5. I pulled on a thick cotton sweater and went outside into the crisp fall day.

6. The cheerful store clerk described the sales to me in a voice that was enthusiastic, melodic, and frankly, a little creepy.

End-of-Unit Assessment

Self-Assessment of My Draft Storyboard

Directions: Today you are turning in your second draft of your Storyboard as your End-of-Unit Assessment. Please answer these questions about your second draft of your Storyboard.

One thing I think I did well in the second draft of my story was . . .

One lingering question or concern I have that I would like my teacher's help on is . . .

Now create a packet that includes the following:

____ Self-Assessment (this piece of paper)

____ Entry Task: Looking at the Rubric (handout from Lesson 8)

____ I Heart Revisions Worksheet (last added to in Lesson 8)

____ Children's Book Storyboards—with first and second draft of text and a sketched-out illustration idea on each page

	3	2	1	Teacher Feedback
Content				
Narrative techniques				
Conventions				
Revisions				

Overall comment:

EXPEDITIONARY
LEARNING

Entry Task

My Final Revisions

1. Read through your storyboards from start to finish and look at the teacher feedback.
2. Stop and think about what you would like to revise for the final draft of your children's story.
3. Write a short paragraph describing the feedback you received and your plan for revision on the I Heart Revisions worksheet.

Turning the Page: Frederick Douglass Learns to Read Matching Cards

(Alternate)

Time: around the time Frederick is eight years old Place: Baltimore Characters: Frederick, Mr. Auld, Mrs. Auld, Thomas, boy in the alley	Mr. Auld finds Mrs. Auld teaching Frederick to read and forbids it. Therefore Frederick realizes that reading is the path to freedom. Learning to read is an important type of freedom.
Frederick finds a boy in the alley.	Frederick has a plan to learn to read.
Frederick versus Mr. Auld Frederick versus society (searching for a way out of slavery)	Frederick convinces the boy to help him learn to read.
Frederick is hopeful for the future because he sees his path to freedom.	Mrs. Auld introduces Frederick to reading.

How a Narrative Is Different from a Summary Reference Sheet

(Alternate)

Example from *Turning the Page*	A Narrative . . .		A Summary . . .
There are many examples. Here is one: "The next morning instead of offering to read to him after breakfast, she said, 'Boy, run out and get the firewood. Don't be lazy!'" (page 14)	"Shows" the most important events unfolding by using sensory description, strong verbs, and dialogue	**Climbing** steps: Tells the story in logical sequence Has a clear climax	Names the important points of action Uses some description and strong verbs
"Arriving at the Auld's door . . ." (page 6) "A few weeks later . . ." (page 16)	Uses transitional words such as *then, next,* and so on		Uses transitional words such as *then, next,* and so on
"That night, Frederick couldn't sleep. Mr. Auld's words kept replaying in his head." (page 12)	Focuses on thoughts and emotions of the character		Mentions thoughts and emotions of characters in passing
"Frederick opened it with trembling hands." (page 20) "Later, as Frederick returned to the Auld's home, he was filled with hope about his new plan. He knew Mrs. Auld would be waiting, ready to lash out at him. But beyond the Aulds, beyond Baltimore, he could see the vast, open sea, wild and full of promise." (page 20)	Shows the resolution of the conflict Shows character growth Implies a theme or universal truth but usually does not explicitly say it	Provides a **conclusion**	Sums up the events of the story Names the resolution of the conflict Directly states character growth and change

Entry Task

Summing It Up

(Alternate)

Name: ____________________

Date: ____________________

Part I

Directions: Complete this task individually.

From *Turning the Page: Frederick Douglass Learns to Read*:

"Later, as Frederick returned to the Auld's home, he was filled with hope about his new plan. He knew Mrs. Auld would be waiting, ready to lash out at him. But beyond the Aulds, beyond Baltimore, he could see the vast, open sea, wild and full of promise."

1. What is the theme that Frederick reflects on in these last few lines?

   ____

2. The sea that is "vast," "open," "wild," and "full of promise" is symbolic to him. Think about those adjectives. What does the sea represent to Frederick?

   ____

Part II

Directions: With a partner, articulate a thematic statement for two of the episodes we read as a class.

Episode:	Episode:
Later, as Frederick walked home, he was filled with ______. He knew that ______ would be waiting for him. But beyond that, out of sight, but near, was the ______ ______ ______ ______.	Later, as Frederick walked home, he was filled with ______. He knew that ______ would be waiting for him. But beyond that, out of sight, but near, was the ______ ______ ______ ______.

My Children's Book Plan
(Alternate)

Name: ______________________________

Date: ______________________________

Directions:

Now you will plan your children's story. When you begin writing, use this plan as a guide. You will probably make small adjustments as you write. As you plan, think carefully about where you will zoom in and be more detailed; do it deliberately and only in moments of the story that need to be examined closely. You may have six to eight pages in your book. You must have at least five pages planned for the Writer's Roundtable tomorrow.

Gist of the story:

____

Thematic statement:

____

____

Page	**Gist of the text** *Narrative tool I will use	**Gist of illustration** (*Remember:* Not every page needs an illustration. Choose the pages that best lend themselves to images.)	**Step on the narrative arc**
Model 4	*FD arrives in Baltimore* * *Sensory details: "carriages, wagons and carts clattered by," "scent of the sea"—put reader in Baltimore* * *Showing character traits: FD wonders whether different might be better—he longs for a different life*	*The wharf scene in Baltimore*	*Establishing context—setting, character, and one of the central conflicts—his longing for a different life*

EXPEDITIONARY
LEARNING

1			
2			
3			
4			
5			
6			
7			

Sharpening Your Tools, Part 1

Show-Not-Tell and Sensory Details

(Alternate)

From *Turning the Page: Frederick Douglass Learns to Read*

One windy afternoon, Frederick arrived in Baltimore harbor on a ship packed with sheep. As he climbed onto the wharf, he could already tell that life here would be different. People of every shade hurried by, well-dressed and full of purpose. Carriages, wagons, carts all clattered by, packed with goods. With the salty scent of the sea, even the air smelled different. Different might mean better, Frederick thought. He couldn't imagine a life worse than the one he'd left behind.

1. What sensory details establish setting?

____

____

"Hello, dear," said Mrs. Auld, with a gentle smile. Frederick could barely reply. Never had a White person spoken to him with such warmth.

2. What character does the author zoom in on? Why is that character important?

____

____

3. The author could just have told us that Mrs. Auld was kind. Instead she *showed* she was kind (an adjective) by using a noun and verb. What noun? What verb phrase shows she is kind?

____

____

Tell (uses bland adjectives)	Show (use nouns and verbs and vivid adjectives)
Mr. Auld was controlling.	
Frederick was scared.	

Sharpening Your Tools, Part 2

Entry Task

(Alternate)

Name: ______________________________

Date: ______________________________

Directions: Read the following paragraphs. They both narrate the same event from *Turning the Page*.

Version 1

The next morning, instead of offering to read to him after breakfast, she said, "Boy, run out and get the firewood. Don't be lazy!" It was the first time Mrs. Auld had talked to him with such coldness, and he felt something inside him being twisted and squeezed.

The days became weeks, and Mrs. Auld became more and more intent on undoing what she had done. Whenever he moved slowly, she yelled at him. Whenever he touched a book, she snatched it away.

It was too late. In introducing Frederick to reading, Mrs. Auld had lit a spark she could never put out. Each time she yelled at him, she only fanned the flames. He might have lost his teacher, but he was determined to find a way to learn to read.

Version 2

The next morning, Mrs. Auld was mean to him. Frederick felt sad and confused. Over the next couple of months she kept being mean. But that didn't discourage Frederick. He still wanted to learn to read.

1. Which version do you think is more clear and vivid, and better helps the reader understand what is happening? Why?

____

____

____

____

2. Which narrative tools do you see the author using in these paragraphs?

____

____

____

____

Sharpening Your Tools: Side-by-Side Comparison
(Alternate)

Version 1	Version 2	
The next morning, instead of offering to read to him after breakfast, she said, "Boy, run out and get the firewood. Don't be lazy!"	The next morning, Mrs. Auld was mean to him.	Precise description: Using "instead of offering to read to him after breakfast" instead of "morning" Precise description: Using dialogue instead of "was mean to him"
It was the first time Mrs. Auld had talked to him with such coldness, and he felt something inside him being twisted and squeezed.	Frederick felt sad and confused.	Sensory word: twisted, squeezed, coldness Precise description: Using "he felt something being twisted and squeezed" instead of "sad and confused"
The days became weeks and Mrs. Auld became more and more intent on undoing what she had done. Whenever he moved slowly, she yelled at him. Whenever he touched a book, she snatched it away.	Over the next couple of months she kept being mean.	Precise description: Using "more intent on undoing what she had done" instead of "kept being mean" Strong verb: snatched
It was too late. In introducing Frederick to reading, Mrs. Auld had lit a spark she could never put out. Each time she yelled at him, she only fanned the flames. He might have lost his teacher, but he was determined to find a way to learn to read.	But that didn't discourage Frederick. He still wanted to learn to read.	Strong verbs: lit, fanned Precise description: he was "determined to find a way to learn to read" instead of "wanted to learn to read"

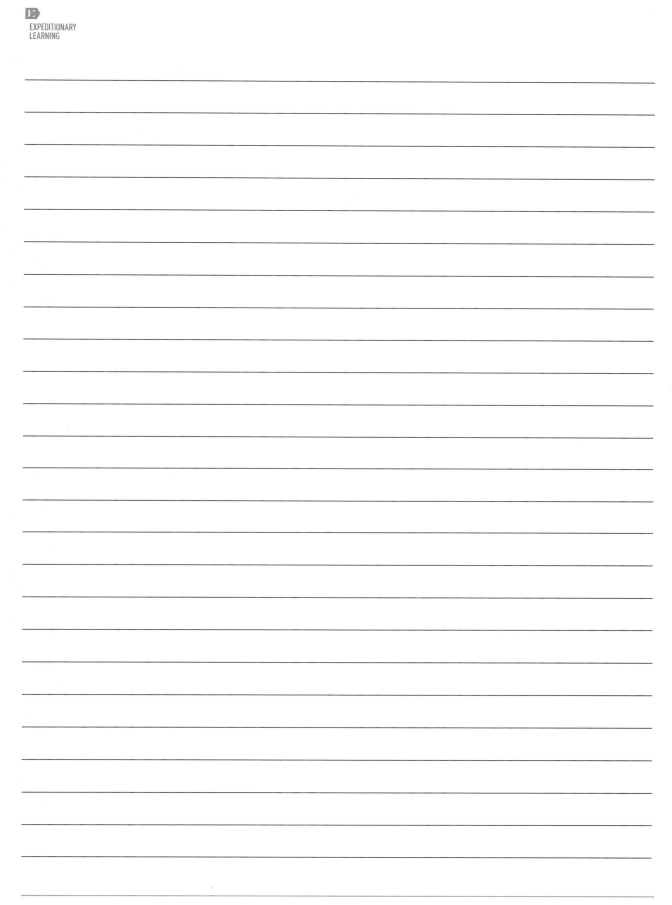